Behavioural Approaches to Corporate Governance

T0295858

Corporate governance failures are all too frequent, and their patterns and outcomes seem avoidably familiar. This book examines the findings of behavioural finance and economics that are most relevant to governance problems, and suggests potential solutions that are best suited to real-world practice and circumstance.

There is a great deal of existing theory that claims to predict the causes and effects of poor governance, and provide solutions. However, the implementation of such measures seems to do little more than merely delay inevitable crises. This book develops a synthesis framework to examine the relative strengths and weaknesses of a behavioural versus deductive approach to understanding the failures of governance. It concludes with a discussion of how corporate governance theory may need to shift going forward, perhaps to include a 'heterodox' ecosystem of theoretical paradigms.

This book will be of interest to students, researchers and practitioners concerned with corporate governance, economic theory and behavioural economics.

Cameron Elliott Gordon is Adjunct Associate Professor, Health Research Institute, University of Canberra, Australia and Principal Investigator, Social Policy Simulation Center/CUNY High Performance Computing Center, City University of New York.

Routledge Advances in Behavioural Economics and Finance
Edited by Richard Fairchild
University of Bath, UK

Behavioural Economics and Business Ethics
Interrelations and Applications
Alexander Rajko

Bounded Rationality and Behavioural Economics
Graham Mallard

Behavioural Approaches to Corporate Governance
Cameron Elliott Gordon

Behavioural Approaches to Corporate Governance

Cameron Elliott Gordon

Routledge
Taylor & Francis Group

LONDON AND NEW YORK

First published 2016 by Routledge

2 Park Square, Milton Park, Abingdon, Oxfordshire OX14 4RN
711 Third Avenue, New York, NY 10017

Routledge is an imprint of the Taylor & Francis Group, an informa business

First issued in paperback 2018

British Library Cataloguing in Publication Data
A catalogue record for this book is available from the British Library

Library of Congress Cataloging in Publication Data
Gordon, Cameron Elliott.
Behavioural Approaches to Corporate Governance / Cameron Elliott
Gordon.
Includes bibliographical references and index.
1. Corporate governance--Psychological aspects. 2. Economics--
Psychological aspects. I. Title.
HD2741.G6696 2015
338.601'9--dc23
2015018881]

ISBN: 978-1-138-80023-6 (hbk)
ISBN: 978-1-138-61139-9 (pbk)

Typeset in Times
by Saxon Graphics Ltd, Derby

Contents

Illustrations

Figure

Tables

1   Introduction

Why is it that corporate governance fails so spectacularly and so regularly? The now receding Global Financial Crisis (GFC) was a complex of many things but not least it was caused by a whole set of companies that seemed to have lost economic and operational common sense. Bad enough, but why didn't any of the governance structures these companies had at least stopgap this collective retreat from reality?

That mega-crisis (arguably not yet resolved) was preceded by the many smaller (but not small) blow-ups such as those of the 'dot-com bubble' at the turn of the current millennium and some spectacular individual corporate governance fiascos associated with the tech boom and associated share price over-runs, including Enron, Worldcom and Tyco, to name several US examples. The Enron scandal also claimed the accounting firm of Arthur Andersen, which showed how corrupted the supposed bedrock of independent auditors had become. A comparable wave of corporate blunders shook the UK a little earlier, in the 1980s and early 1990s. Europe had its own scandals during this first decade of the new millennium, including the spectacular implosion of the Italian conglomerate Parmalat.

But of course corporate governance scandals and failures go back much farther than this. The 1980s in the US saw the rise of the 'corporate raiders', 'hostile takeover', and 'leveraged buyouts' (LBOs) that were sometimes, if not often, of questionable ethics and value, inspiring movies like 'Wall Street', stage shows like 'Other People's Money' and books like 'Barbarians at the Gate' the last of which tracked one of the most notorious of LBOs, the RJR-Nabisco deal. The 1980s were also the era of the Savings and Loans crisis in the US which ended in the biggest government banking bailout up to that time. The UK was seeing some similar upheaval during this time of its own 'Big Bang' deregulation of financial markets, culminating at the end of the decade with the 1990 Polly Peck collapse which inspired the 1992 Cadbury Report. Although this report was said to have reformed British corporate governance, it certainly did not stop the GFC from shaking that country.

And these are only the last 40 years. The Great Depression of the 1930s is the penultimate major crisis, the cataclysm that has served as the template for policy-makers who have sought to avoid its policy and governance mistakes. Just as

World War 1 was once known as the 'war to end all wars', the Great Depression, it was hoped, was the depression to end all depressions. But it has not turned out that way and the reforms that the GFC has inspired have not inspired confidence that there is any permanent solution for the 'madness of crowds', to use Charles Mackay's popular phrase (Mackay 1841/2002).

The era between World War 2 and the mid-1970s has faded into memory as a relatively peaceful, prosperous and stable corporate world. Indeed, large corporate failures with the taint of governance malfunction were relatively few during this period (the sudden surprise bankruptcy of the Penn Central Railroad in 1970 in the US being one notable exception). Widespread prosperity certainly helped, for these decades witnessed an early experiment with financial and corporate organisational engineering in the form of the corporate conglomeration movement. Penn Central was a prominent victim of this but others, such as the iconic symbol of the movement, ITT (formerly the International Telephone and Telegraph company), were seen as share value underperformers and very likely may have failed in the more turbulent decades to come. The UK's economic picture was certainly more turbulent in this era, especially with the currency crisis and extreme labour unrest that marked the epoch right before the first oil price shock spoiled things for everyone. But the dominant tone there was not one of corporate failure so much as government, union and geopolitical distress. If only things could be run as well as a business, things would not be so bad, so the thinking went, later triumphing in a wave of 'neo-liberalism' through the developed world.

If, however, one thinks there are ideological solutions to corporate governance conundrums, one only has to see that they occur whatever the stripe of regime in power. One could telegraph this history back into the Great Depression, the oligarchic economic structures of the late 19th century with its trusts and relatively frequent economic crashes and go further back to the South Sea Bubble and Tulipmania. The point should be clear: human business enterprises are prone to failure. Of course failure in business is inevitable and corporate collapses typically have varied causes, especially since commerce is an inherently risky affair. But some failures are clearly avoidable, and many are driven by what in retrospect seems to be clear human folly, or at least very bad judgement, typically accompanied by malfunction in the way that the entity was managed and controlled; in short, defective corporate governance.

Many have studied the causes and effects of these problems and many are studying them still. This book does consider some of this literature but its objectives are a bit different than creating a manual of good practice or of theoretical unassailability. The focus instead is on two things: (1) 'classical' corporate governance theory and its 'neoclassical' economic foundations; and (2) the relatively new 'behavioural' strain in economics and the implications this variant may have for corporate governance design and prescription. There is a good deal of literature on behavioural social science but relatively little that is applied to the field of institutional governance as yet and this book is designed to fill that current gap.

Of course there is more than just the economic theory of corporate governance and the relative lack of focus on these other views is not meant to indicate that these are not relevant, important or useful. The fact is, however, that economic theory has implicitly and explicitly dominated corporate governance analysis, practice and policy prescriptions over the past four decades at least (before that more heterodoxy was evident, especially during the Great Depression). Thus it is important to summarise what this theory says and what its limits are.

Because mainstream economics is now transfixed with a set of specific behavioural observations and ideas, it is also important to know what these observations consist of and how they have changed, and more importantly, not changed economic theory, with a look at how this then affects the corporate governance paradigm that flows from that theory.

Since corporate governance is fundamentally something to be practiced, this book moves from a theoretical foundation to seeing how current governance practices might be modified, according to the findings of behavioral economics, and, most critically, whether these changes would actually make much difference. The book concludes with a discussion of next frontiers in both theory and policy.

Having been trained as an economist in a largely neoclassical mode, this author is aware of the strengths of that form of economic theory and its legitimate uses. But the argument will be made that the 'standard' economic theory foundation of corporate governance, while strong in some ways, has more than met its limits in the corporate governance field and that the behavioural version of the theory, while an improvement in some ways, is nonetheless much more modest than many of its practitioners claim it to be.

It will be argued that it is really time for a comprehensive rethink of corporate governance ideas that incorporate other variants of economics and ideas and insights from other disciplines. Some of the current economic model certainly should be retained but much of it needs to be discarded and replaced, much as astronomers and navigators using Ptolemy's model of planetary movements ultimately saw their increasingly epicycle-ridden calculations overthrown by the observations of Kepler, Copernicus, Galileo and then the theories of Newton (which, in fundamental but not practical terms has itself been supplanted by Relativity Theory and quantum mechanics).

I will return to this analogy in the last chapter on new frontiers where some basic methodological points have to be grappled with since the bulk of economists claim that 'it takes a theory to beat a theory' and that they use the clean and spare principles of Newton though in fact, in my view, are using a Ptolemaic construct. If the economics profession hopes to remain truly relevant, at least in the governance and associated policy arena, it has to recognise and correct some fundamental conceptual problems. Otherwise economics may well be overthrown and if so, as with most revolutions, a lot of good will go out with the bad.

Whether one agrees with the critique or not, the core of the book provides a reference on both theory and practice in standard and behavioural corporate governance and some suggestions for new and approaches to governance that take into account known human psychological characteristics.

2 'Neoclassical' corporate governance theory

Corporate governance as generally practised in the developed world rests on an underlying theory of economics generally referred to as 'neoclassical'. Thus the discussion here will refer to 'neoclassical' Governance Theory. To understand more about the implications of behavioural economics for corporate governance, one must first understand explicitly what the traditional model of governance entails and the nature of its neoclassical economic roots.

Anglo-American Economic Theory as developed in the late 19th century through much of the 20th century posits a number of strong simplifying assumptions and concepts about the economy, creating an idealised world in which economic behaviour can theoretically be easily modelled and predicted. This ideal world consists of actors who all share the characteristics of being 'rational', 'maximising' 'selfish' and 'atomistic'. These terms actually have varying meanings across the literature and are not always tightly defined. But one can define these terms broadly as follows.

- 'Rational' refers to a well-ordered thought and decision-making process and a consistent set of personal preferences.
- 'Maximising' refers to the preference held by each actor to have and consume more of a preferred good rather than less, with no obvious limiting satiation point.
- 'Selfish' refers to each Agent's objective of ensuring one's own welfare is tended to and optimised before anyone else's.
- 'Atomistic' is a state in which each actor is unrelated to any other actor except through transactions each might choose to conduct with one another.

Goods and services in this world are not desired for their innate or inherent properties but because they contribute to an actor's overall satisfaction. The economics term for satisfaction is 'utility' and whatever an actor consumes enters into their individual 'utility function'. This function, which is a pure theoretical construct, not actually observable, is posited to be a sort of internal individual 'technology' that converts consumption items into individual utility (satisfaction). This is why the word 'function' is used because just as a mathematical equation takes given numerical inputs and transforms them into different numerical outputs, a utility function transforms consumption inputs into consumer utility.

The exact nature of this process is said to vary from individual to individual and is often simply expressed generically, e.g. as something like $U_n = f(C_n)$ where U_n refers to the utility of actor 'n', C_n refers to the consumption of actor 'n' and f refers to the function (technology) that converts consumption into utility for the actor. There can be more than one 'argument' (input) in a utility function and usually is. For example more detailed classes of consumption items might be specified, a broad example being C, as before, and L, for leisure time. Or it is possible that the consumption or utility of other actors might be included. Maybe actor 'n' is a father who cares about how much consumption his daughter, actor 'm' has and so an argument C_m might be included as well as C_n.

The theorist then might specify a particular functional form, e.g. $U_n = 10 + C_n$, and one plugs in units of C to arrive at total U. If actor 'n' consumes 20 units of C, total utility for that actor equals 30 'utils' (which is often how individual units of utility are referred to), obviously calculated from $10 + 20 = 30$. This example is arbitrary and usually specific functions are more elaborate and typically said to be arrived at from supposedly plausible assumptions that accord with empirically validated findings often referred to as 'stylised facts' and also which accord with the more general behavioural assumptions of the neoclassical economic model.

These assumptions have already been noted. Their implications for a utility function go like this. As everyone is a maximiser, everyone seeks, by definition, to get as much utility as they can given their individual resource constraints and the relative market prices of desired goods in the marketplace at the time. Since actors are selfish they conduct their utility maximisation calculations from their own vantage point. Since they are rational, their utility calculations are not arbitrary and are logical in a general sense and all their actions are based on these calculations. Since they are atomistic they calculate solely on the basis of their individual utility maximisation and when they interact with other parties in the market they treat others as either constraints to, or as providers of inputs into, that.

Individual versions of models based on these assumptions differ from one another in certain ways and there is actually room for fairly wide variation in the technical and natural language meaning of these terms. For example, 'selfish' in some theoretical treatments can refer to an actor whose utility function includes other actors close to one's self, such as children (which in a sense modifies the assumption of atomism, though neoclassical economists do not see things in this way). And 'rational' can cover a multitude of internal thinking and calculating processes. And these assumptions do not need imply that all actors are 'identical' in terms of things like their preferences or even their processes. Some particular conceptions do posit this (technically imposing identical utility functions shared by all actors, for example) but others do not and it is not strictly necessary to assume identical actor preferences to have an economic model which fits the neoclassical mould and functions as such.

The bottom-line is that Neoclassical Economic Theory is a flexible one that shares some basic general assumptions to create a conceptual reality capable of yielding predictions that can be measured against empirical reality. These are still, however, highly idealised simplifying assumptions. Not even all economists accept these limitations of and no less a figure than economics Nobel Prize winner Amartya Sen has noted how 19th century theorists who posited some of these extremes in the quest for formal simplification hoped that they would be superseded and has explored some ways to modify and expand the assumptions of neoclassical theory (Sen 1977).

It should also be clear that the model gains a lot of power through its generality. But this same generality can lead to both the risk of tautology and a lack of clarity about empirical validation. For example, since rationality can cover a wide variety of internal reasoning processes, it can be difficult to say whether the actual data are consistent or inconsistent with the assumption of actor rationality. This issue and others will be considered in more detail later on.

So where does corporate governance fit into this model? One accepted definition of corporate governance (one of many) is: "Procedures and processes according to which an organisation is directed and controlled. The corporate governance structure specifies the distribution of rights and responsibilities among the different participants in the organisation – such as the board, managers, shareholders and other stakeholders – and lays down the rules and procedures for decision-making (OECD 2005).

Defined this way there does not immediately appear to be any logical necessity for including corporate governance in the rarefied neoclassical world. Since actors are completely atomistic and transactional, while temporary alliances may well arise between individuals because there are mutual gains from trade and coordination, there is no obvious reason for any actor to create new structures or organisations that are separate and apart and which require governance. In fact the creation of artificial entities entails the use of scarce resources such as time and energy that would be better put directly into consumption of utility increasing goods, at least in this model.

Yet organisations and their need for governance and oversight are widely observed in the real world. The Neoclassical Economic Theory therefore spawned a neoclassical governance model to explain, on its own terms, why organisations exist and how to best govern such organisations. This model consists of three major conceptual building blocks, as follows.

1 The assumption of an Agency Problem (which arises from Principal–Agent Theory).
2 Transactions Costs Economics (TCE).
3 Contracting Theory.

These three legs make up the neoclassical corporate governance stool from which most of the major corporate governance devices used today have their intellectual origins. Each one will now be considered in turn. It should be mentioned that many standard narratives would change the 1-2-3 order above to 2-1-3 as TCE can, in many ways, give birth to the agency problem. The argument here will be that the Agency Problem can be both independent of as well as come from TCE so it will be discussed first.

Economic Theory often uses the word 'Agents' to refer to 'actors' and both terms are used though the former is more common usage. To avoid confusion 'actors' here refer to individuals in the economic model, while 'Agents' are used to refer the Agents as distinguished from 'Principals' in neoclassical Governance Theory.

The agency problem

The traditional theoretical basis of the need for institutions separate from actors and hence the need for institutional governance in the neoclassical economic model is Principal–Agent Theory. Remember that all actors are atomistic, rational, maximising and selfish. Therefore human notions of 'trust' or 'relationship' do not apply. Actors only engage with one another to get something from each other in individual market transactions. Their dynamic is inherently competitive and asocial and perhaps even clinically sociopathic if a psychiatrist were observing.

Whether actors have identical preferences or not they are all out to get the most possible satisfaction and each other actor is a potential barrier to that, though also, of course, a bridge to greater individual and collective utility if gains from trade can be identified and then executed. Thus, of course, actors will often have different interests from one another. There will be many times when actors will find that they are better off trading with one another, the so-called 'mutual gains from trade' familiar from classical economists like Adam Smith and David Ricardo. Yet, by definition, these actors will often be in competition with one another. And even when their interests align, they cannot rely on simple trust to work together for, being selfish maximisers, they cannot be trusted. What to do?

In the pure economic model, with its very rigorous and restricted assumptions the answer lies in the market mechanism. The market, though it is often anthropomorphised (as Smith's term 'The Invisible Hand' indicates), actually does not exist separately from the transactions between actors. Indeed the pure world here is completely nonphysical. There is no time, and actors and their activities occupy no space; in fact there is no space at all, just actors calculating their plans of action based on maximising their individual satisfaction. Actors seek out other actors to transact with to obtain 'inputs' that can be fed into their individual utility functions to increase their individual satisfaction.

This market process automatically aligns interests (actually, preferences; interest is too complex a word in this context) because transactions will not occur at all except when someone has what someone else wants and assuming they can reach an agreed upon price which increases satisfaction on both sides of the transaction. If there is no potential for mutual gain, there will be no transaction and no need of one since all transactions that do occur are 'optimal' in an economic sense since all gain from them. Any transaction that makes one party worse off is not desirable from both an individual point of view and from a society's point of view since in this atomistic world a society is simply the sum of all the individual actors and their transactions.

In the ideal pure model there are also 'many' sellers and buyers and they are selling 'identical' 'goods' to one another. These are everyday terms that evoke common sense images. But remember that this is the world of pure number, much like the world posited by Pythagoras. The actors are disembodied and so are the 'goods'. Moreover, consumers are also producers of goods. So, really there is nothing but a continuing series of pairwise number calculations occurring which yields the highest possible total of satisfaction units (units of utility or 'utils') across actors. We know this will be the highest possible number because this process is 'perfectly competitive' which is to say that all transactions must in the end settle at a price equal exactly to the marginal cost of the unit being sold. No one can oversell at this price because others will instantaneously step in to undercut any price greater than marginal cost and, of course, it is impossible to remain solvent while consistently underselling with a price that does not cover marginal cost of production. The informal references to overselling and underselling are themselves a bit misleading since there is no time in this model. Every possible transaction settles immediately and all at once.

So far, in this world of pure trade there should be no need of governance. But what if some other underlying assumptions are relaxed? A more 'realistic' though still highly abstracted model could posit the following.

- **Imperfect information.** In the pure model it was implicitly assumed that all Agents possessed identical information. One could posit an alternative of information asymmetry, that is, a world where some actors have information others don't, and thus an 'advantage' when it comes to trade. This information could take many forms, one of which is 'expertise' (more properly experience or learning in this context) in a given consumption or production market.
- **Imperfect property rights.** In this virtual world, property rights is a misleading term to use since a good is only an abstract number, not physical property, but individual control over even that number is implicitly inviolate and transferability of that control is seamless from buyer to seller. Perhaps, though, there might now be occasions where transfer of control is not always perfect, especially if the good is somehow inextricably linked to the individual actor, such as 'expertise' and its products.
- **Unequal distribution of actor capabilities and necessary interdependence.** Following from the point above, although actors need not be identical in preference or in what they have to offer each other, it could well be the case that some capabilities are 'indispensable' either globally (e.g. health care) or for particular situations (e.g. language translation services for actors speaking different languages) and these are distributed in such a way in which actors need to rely on other actors in ways that involve interdependence rather than mere series of transactions. Now a situation arises where actors don't just transact with each other but have to depend on one another.

- **Returns to interdependence rather than just gains from individual trade.**
  Which raises the next point: what if actors can gain even more from mutual
  interdependence rather than just trading with one another? In other words
  actors might find they all are better off by joining forces to work together in
  welfare increasing production and consumption rather than merely conducting
  market transactions with one another, at least in some cases. Now the constraint
  of competition is not relevant or even fully useful. But what then stops these
  rapacious untrustworthy actors from consuming each other if they do decide to
  work together? If they cannot overcome this barrier then the market economy
  now is leaving some possible mutual gain on the table and leaving a situation
  where it is possible to make some actors better off without making any of them
  worse off (in technical terms a non-'Pareto' optimality). These maximisers will
  certainly want to devise some way of changing this unsatisfactory situation.

It should be clear that the dimensions of time and physical space and form must
be added to the model for these nuances to make any sense. Put technically the
characteristic of 'embodiment' is now being added to the world of the theory.
Few economic theorists, even behavioural ones, make this explicit but it must be
added to allow for consideration of many real world situations, and it has broader
implications to be discussed further below. One of these implications is that there
is the potential to have two classes of actor arise: Principals and Agents. This is
not how the literature typically states things but this construct is arguably a
foundation for the more traditional statements of the Principal–Agent Problem
which arise from the presence of transactions costs.

In the purely abstract world we started with, transactions were in pure
commodities between actors whose only interactions were market transactions.
We now enter a world with subtle physicality (though not yet, dare it be said, real
humanity) in which some transactions involve exchanges between actors trading
in specialised services that only they possess and which others need and which
require working together in ways not possible in the marketplace alone.

To understand this a bit more, consider a simple model of interdependence with
the presence of embodiment. Say an owner of 'surplus' capital buys a sugar
plantation because that has the highest possible rate of return of all investment
alternatives. But this owner has no expertise in running such a plantation and buys
one which already exists and which is being run by a particular overseer with
maximum skill. These particularities are unimportant, but the example illustrates a
very typical disjoint found in the embodied economic world that real economic
actors live in. We can see that in this case there are two actors in different positions.
We refer to the owner and investor of capital as the 'Principal' and the manager
overseeing the plantation on his or her behalf as the 'Agent'. Both need each other
but neither can trust one another to act in the other's interests.

Why? One could formulate the problem facing these two parties as follows.

The Principal seeks to maximise value received from the Agent's services, i.e.
maximise V which equals: value received from the Agent's services minus the
payment made to the Agent.

The Agent has this problem: maximise V which equals the payment received from the Principal minus the costs to the Agent of providing services.

Since these are rational, maximising and 'atomistic' Agents (in the sense that they are assumed to be acting as if they are totally unrelated to one another, except for their technical interdependence, which is a function of the way some skills and goods are embodied) it is clear that their value maximisation problems are 'misaligned.' The Agent's benefit minus cost margin entails delivering minimum possible service to the Principal in return for maximum payment from him or her, while the Principal wants maximum Agent services in return for as small as possible a payment (Besanko et al. 2007).

What's the 'solution' to this problem? It actually depends upon the exact nature of the transaction. If both the Principals and Agents are trucking in standardised services and goods for which there are deep and competitive markets, the market mechanism should take of the better part of major misalignments. There are many services, e.g. real estate sales, bookkeeping and standard financial auditing, executive placement and recruitment, etc., where Principals can hire Agents to do set tasks on a transaction by transaction basis and rely on competitive markets for those services. The dynamic and wide information base produced by those markets would generally minimise exploitation of Principals by Agents and, conversely, Agents by Principals. Of course in the real world, this will not be perfect and mistakes will be made in some initial cases. But if Agents are to survive in a competitive market they must deliver maximum value at a competitive price and if Principals want to have steady access to Agent value bundles, they cannot exploit or cheat on their Agents more than once or twice.

The problems get bigger as Principal/Agent objectives widen, competitive markets thin out, information asymmetries on either side increase and time and physical reality impinges in particular ways. For the moment let's stick to 'external' Principal–Agent exchanges, i.e. those between unrelated and unaffiliated Agents who transact purely through a market mechanism.

Even in this simple world, Agency problems begin to become less amenable to market solutions as Agent actions become more difficult to observe. A real-estate transaction similar to thousands of others that takes place daily is easy to monitor as far as Agent performance is concerned. But to return to our earlier example of the sugar plantation overseer, suboptimal performance there may be harder to detect, especially if it is relatively small. Maybe there are only a small number of such plantations worldwide and they are not identical to one another. So it is not easy to value the services that the Agent is offering and especially the efficiency with which the Agent is working.

We already assumed that this investment had the highest rate of return. But perhaps the overseer is being a little less efficient than possible, working a few less hours than the Principal is paying for. Remember that the Principal has hired the Agent in this case because they don't know the business well, so there is an information asymmetry and interdependence in this regard. And perhaps there are not many overseers available in the marketplace at any one time, and they don't come available often and all one has to assess outcomes are data on actual performance not optimal performance. Here the misalignment is not entirely corrected by the market. An inefficiency is allowed to persist without further corrective action. Thus some sort of 'governance' solution becomes necessary.

This is a simple and contrived example. Problems such as this increase as the lack of transparency in the market does and this can be caused by factors such as non-tradable goods and services that have no market at all, markets that are thin and not very competitive, and markets that can only handle 'bundles' of services or goods where inefficiency might arise in the delivery of a piece of that bundle (e.g. childcare which consists of individual things like feeding, storytelling, security etc. which are nonetheless most efficiently sold and delivered as a package). In effect there is some kind of 'market failure' occurring in these cases and some sort of nonmarket arrangement might be needed to correct it. Though if the failure's efficiency consequences are small enough and undetectable enough the parties might be more than happy to leave things as they are.

Transactions costs economics (TCE)

Let's make a thus far implicit assumption explicit: there are no transactions costs for Principal/Agent deals. A simple potential solution to the problems identified above is monitoring of Agents by Principals. This won't be perfect because, as noted, there is no longer perfect information. But problems could be minimised if Principals watched their Agents perform all the time and collected as much information on benchmark efficiency as possible to supplement whatever the market is failing to deliver. There would still be issues between Principals and Agents but governance generally would likely be a fairly small problem with fairly small-scale solutions and generally insignificant welfare losses to economic actors.

However, it is recognised that economic transactions are costly in some way, in time and effort at least, and this is where TCE comes in. Many things are born from this relaxation of the implicit assumption that transactions are costless.

The literature on TCE and governance is huge but its primary implication is that the presence of transactions costs create a divide between 'external' transactions and 'internal' ones. Coase (1937) is the progenitor of this theory and he proposed the widely accepted notion that the existence of such costs is the reason that the firm exists. And once the firm is allowed, governance follows as a logical necessity.

If transactions are costless and the rest of the 'perfect' market exists, even with physical time and space, it is not obvious that agents should need to establish organisations. They may depend on one another in negotiated nonmarket deals but these remain transactionally based. Maximum efficiency should be obtainable by actors transacting with each other ad hoc to achieve particular welfare maximising ends and establishing side deals to correct incentives for unperformance by Agents where a Principal–Agent problem arises.

Even very large and complex transactions, e.g. building an aircraft carrier or educating the masses, would seem to be best addressed on a transaction by transaction basis in the neoclassical model, even where there is embodiment and asymmetric information. Any undertaking involving collective (private) action can be reduced to the necessary pairwise gains from mutual trade, just added up to the whole that makes up the sum of the parts. It is true that there may now be 'second-best' outcomes where information asymmetries allow for persistent inefficiencies. But it is hard to see the need for formal organisation besides market deals. Granted, these deals might be continually renewed for a very long period of time and might have a scale and scope of coordination that appears to be organisational. But no separate entity is there. Once the deals stop, the organised effort stops and this could happen instantaneously.

However, if transactions now are assumed to have even small costs, there will be cases where Agents will want to work together with Principals in more stable and long-lived arrangements to minimise overall transactions costs. The existence of the firm now can be justified as a transaction-cost minimising strategy rather than an inexplicable *deus ex machina* that just happens to occur in reality. There are other philosophical bases for explaining the firm's presence, but from a neoclassical perspective this is the logical one and simplest since most of the rest of the economic model can be left untouched.

The decision to build an organisation thus boils down to this: if the total cost of completing transactions for a given objective (total transactions costs) is greater than the total of the net gains of the transactions, then it will be welfare increasing for all involved to establish a entity, separate from the market and from the individual actors, to manage these mutually beneficial trades assuming the entity's own costs are less than the total transactions costs incurred through a bundle of individual trades. In other words, parties to an enterprise will all be better off creating a non-market entity to conduct 'internal' transactions when these internal costs are less than conducting business through individual market trades.

Now we have the cleaving of earth from the waters. On the Second Day TCE made 'internal' and 'external' markets from what was one the day before.

This exposition is highly simplified, of course. But the fundamental problem and its theoretical solution is laid bare. A good deal is, as will be seen later, unstated and unclear however. For example, why should truly atomistic greedy Agents stick together within an organisation or be able to really agree to create one at all, even when there are clear potential mutual gains? It is not at all clear what makes a firm coalesce or, once coalesced, remain stable.

Indeed firms even in this more nuanced neoclassical world would seem to be more like classic cartels, carefully balanced between individual mistrust and mutual incentive to stick together, prone to internal collapse at a moment's notice. This is not what is typically observed in the vast majority of corporate forms. Still, there is a lot of power in this definition of the problem and a lot of Corporate Governance Theory has clear justification on its basis.

And there is now a firm and this firm has 'internal' incentives within its boundaries. 'Externally', the firm is subject to the pressures of the marketplace. But the providers of capital have calculated that their returns are better if they stand together and pool their resources to create this new entity, the firm, than if they stand alone. Their firm is now established and ready to go. But how does it run and what ensures it reaches its desired destination? It now stands as a separate entity with its own internal dynamics, bounded though they may be. Principals still need to manage the firm and they bring Agents in to do so, doing a lot of things internally and therefore outside the normal 'self-regulating' processes of the markets. Governance of the firm's internal workings is now an immediate concern whose design and execution is critical.

Putting aside for now the underlying property rights framework, which becomes more complicated once we allow legal entities separate from individual Agents and Principals, there are two basic governance structures to consider. The first is the structure or organisational form of the firm. The second is the design of the implicit and explicit contracts that govern the relationship between Principal and Agent.

The structure, or form, chosen for the company is the foundation of the corporate entity. Some economists call this 'organisational architecture' and, as the term implies, some conscious and intentional design is required, as distinct from the impersonal workings of the market's 'invisible hand' (Brickley et al. 2001).

Remember that our theoretical economic actors and their basic characteristics are the same whether working in a market or within a firm. They are selfish, maximising, atomistic and rational in either setting. But the economic problem is more subtle and difficult within the firm than outside in the pure competitive market. A key challenge is to design an entity where efficient control and coordination of activities within it can be accomplished without the use of standard market price and competitive allocation methods.

The design problem requires getting right the structure of organisation coordination of internal firm activities, especially the flow of information to ensure achievement of objectives, and control, which requires setting the location of decision-making and rule-making authority within a hierarchy. These design tasks apply to all levels within the firm: individual, team and organisational levels. Within the neoclassical framework the criteria for design success is a result where structures minimise transactions costs and align Principal and Agent incentives as effectively as possible.

From an economist's single-minded perspective, all the observed varieties of corporate form arise from the balance between minimisation of transactions costs with the necessary mobilisation of resources to maximise competitive advantage and profitability of the firm in the marketplace, particularly decisions pertaining to firm integration across a value stream including vertical/horizontal, upstream/ downstream and make/buy (sourcing) decisions (Williamson 1985).

Armen Alchian and Harold Demsetz (1972) make this argument explicitly, stating that the firm exists because beyond a certain size individual and self-managed team effort in markets is not sufficient to achieve business goals. Coordination and control of Agents is needed past that point when atomistic ad hoc transactions become too costly to control and coordinate without a larger formal entity established outside the market. This trade-off not only brings the firm into being; it also affects how the firm structures itself and how it evolves over time.

Paul Milgrom and John Roberts (1992) coined the term 'influence costs' in this context to refer to the cost of management activity devoted to lobbying within organisations to allocate internal nonmarket resources to various uses. In other words, once Principals provide capital to a firm, it becomes 'internal capital' and its allocation within the firm has an obviously political flavour, indicating that as far as pure theory is concerned we are not in a perfect market setting where such things are driven out by 'perfect' economic forces (although obviously the firm itself is subject to market pressures and this sets outer bounds on internal firm decisions). Milgrom and Roberts claim that influence costs will be higher for some organisational forms than others and that this, balanced against task- and mission-efficient cost and benefit drivers, will result in a choice of form that hopefully maximises net benefit for the firm.

It should be obvious that the choice of form will evolve as costs and benefits shift. There is no one optimal structure since contextual factors are so important. But the relatively few variations of corporate form observed in the real world do suggest some inherently limiting design factors.

Firm structure and form is important but it is not the same thing as governance of that form. One can design a good watertight ship but if the captain sails it into an iceberg all that design is for naught. Still, form does interplay with governance in critical ways. Some of the key questions in this area include the following:

- What are the limits to structural change driven by innate economic characteristics of organisational activity?
- How can structure/form act as a means of information cost minimisation and management?
- In what ways does structure serve as both a means of executing market strategy and a key driver in shaping it?
- How does corporate form evolve in a dynamic and changing environment?

A truncated catalogue of some answers to these questions is presented below.

- John Roberts (2004) has argued that organisational design variables are inherent complements or substitutes for one another and this fact limits effective mix and match of forms. In other words much as a certain number of hammers requires a certain number of nails to be obtained (a complementary relationship) or having a certain number of laptop computers available limits the need to acquire desktop computers (a substitute relationship), corporate form has a relatively limited set of useful designs, even though the theoretical possibilities are nearly limitless. An example would be a tall hierarchical form which might require lots of direct control mechanisms but relatively few coordination mechanisms because authority is clustered at the top and the 'troops' just need to follow orders, and not know much more than that.

- Some theories of structure focus on information cost and flow as a prime causal factor. Galbraith and Kazanjian (1986) argue that work groups of actors can normally work independently with developed 'routines' but that as exceptions arise more administrative staff are needed to handle these and this increases and changes the shape of hierarchy.

- Along similar lines, Stinchcombe (1990) argues that firms should organise to maximise efficient information retrieval where this is especially important to their value chain. For example, a large pharmaceutical firm may wish to establish an independent pharmaceutical R&D department capable of rapid coordination with others for new product development, a critical part of its core business which requires special attention and nimble, flexible response not tied down by the overall corporate hierarchy. Kogut and Zander (1993) argue analogously that the multinational form has emerged as an efficient information processing form relative to others as value chains have internationalised.

- An old business debate revolves around corporate strategy and its relationship to form. Alfred Chandler (1962) argued famously that structure follows strategy, and most have agreed with him. In other words, a business value proposition is formulated, a decision is made to establish a firm to prosecute this proposition in the market and a corporate form is chosen which is thought to be the most efficient way of doing that.

- However some, like Hammond (1996), argue for a two-way street, with structure having effects on strategy which then feeds back into structure. He claims that information retrieval, processing and decision-making capabilities are widely distributed in large firms and that this furnishes proof that the company form is as much about taking information in and changing with respect to it as much as it is about putting information and strategy out into the world.

- This sort of reasoning is the stuff of evolutionary economics (which will be encountered again later on). For there can be little question that organisation structure affects and can bias information, and other resource flows, in critical ways. Nelson and Winter (1982) take an evolutionary economics approach to claim strategy and structure are simplifying 'routines' in which the former is a set of routines adapted for survival and growth while the latter is a set adapted for coordinating firm responses to everyday changes in the environment and achievement of necessary tasks.

- Moving further down the hierarchy, Burt (1992) puts forward a structural holes theory in which one actor serves as a critical link to others in a network and thus gathers power (which is implicit and distinguished from authority, which is explicit) within a particular form. He further looks at how actor behaviour may change within the form itself and vice-versa. Just as forms have variations on a theme, so does actor behaviour.

These are all economic theories of structure and obviously not the only approach to this wide-ranging topic. What is interesting is that there have been economists who predate the behavioural economics movement yet have come up with some predictions and concepts consistent or similar to it, as shall be seen in the following chapters.

The other point to be made is that a lot of variety arises from the relatively simple, yet flexible assumptions of the neoclassical economic model. However, is there a dominant solution or do all of these occur and co-exist? If so, while the neoclassical model generates nice tight stories, it is not clear that it can be reliably falsified, a concern also directed at evolutionary approaches to corporate governance. In other words, much variety can is observed in the corporate world and the neoclassical model can be said to be consistent with all of it. But how good is such a theory? This methodological issue will be revisited many times in the course of the discussion.

Contracting theory

With the presence of the Agency Problem and the friction of transactions costs the need for negotiated agreement, implicit and explicit, between actors is clear. Competitive market forces cannot be used, or at least used efficiently, in cases where these two things exist. The firm is a means to an end and its design is critical. But once in operation, what vehicle can be used to ensure that the Agents do their jobs and do them well? Contracting Theory suggests the answer: contracts.

Contracts in a legal sense are binding agreements between parties toward achieving specific agreed upon ends and often using specifically agreed upon means. More generally a contract is any agreement between parties that is potentially enforceable, by law or other means, of delivering rewards and punishment for degrees of compliance and noncompliance with its terms.

It is probably only a small simplification to say that contracting is the primary method (outside of the background workings of corporate form) that neoclassical Economic Theory offers as a solution to the Agency Problem and its associated information asymmetries and uncertainty. Neoclassical Governance Theory is mostly about design and enforcement of contracts within the firm and between firms. Such contracts can be implicit or explicit or a mix of both. They can also be embedded in institutions and rules and here the boundaries between form and contracts can get a bit blurred. The key challenge overall is to design contract terms and incentives properly, ensure that institutional arrangements are concordant with these incentives and then add enforcement and compliance structures as needed, though preferably on as limited a basis as possible since the market mechanism is considered the ideal welfare maximiser.

A key concept that arises in this literature is 'optimal' which can be defined as an outcome where net private benefits are maximised. ('Externalities' – that is, costs or benefits not internalised by the firm or the market but placed on the larger society, such as pollution – are not considered in this basic framework but are accommodated in extensions to the model. These are important but outside the scope of this discussion.) 'Optimality' is closely related to the notion of 'efficiency' which indicates an allocation of resources in which the sum total of material resources available is such that no one can be made better off without someone being made worse off (as noted above, referred to as 'Pareto optimality' after the Italian economist who invented the concept).

In these terms, and to oversimplify a bit, governance design and implementation can be reduced to a constrained optimisation problem in which there is an economic allocation of resources given scarcity of these resources that cannot be improved upon materially at any given point in time (Shliefer and Vishny 1997). In other words, this theory suggests that it is always possible to identify and define some kind of economic optimum, at least theoretically, and that this economic optimum is always the desired goal to work towards. (Interestingly this is an idea that is held by the behavioural economics paradigm as well, a point to be returned later on and one that indicates that paradigm to be more incremental than some claim it to be). Issues of implicit values and morality within the model itself (for example, the 'more is better' goal implied by maximisation) and more general ethical notions such as fairness are sidelined or unacknowledged. It will be argued later on that these can have serious consequences in the corporate governance arena.

The issue of 'completeness' of contracts now arises. In the real world all relevant contingencies and performance outcomes cannot be specified and/or enforcement of terms cannot be perfect unless one is in the rarefied and highly formalised realm of Arrow and Debreu (1954) in which literally every possible aspect of reality across all time periods can be measured and evaluated and put into contract terms. In practice incomplete contracts are the norm and governance consists of determining the appropriate incentives for all relevant Agents and Principals and then designing contract terms which capture those incentives as fully as possible and provide exactly the right rewards and punishments to induce economically efficient performance on all sides. It should be obvious that this can be a tall order in all but an ideal world.

Specific contracts have a basis in general contract law, which is legislated formally, or otherwise provided for informally. Just as individual contracts will be incomplete, background contract law itself will be too. This is due to a number of factors: information will never be complete, both in the present (asymmetries) and in the future (uncertainties); information may be private or propriety and thus unavailable to all parties even if it exists somewhere in the system; contract law itself will evolve in ways that cannot always be foreseen; and natural language itself, the stuff of contracts and law, has ambiguity, an important limit to exact performance specifications; finally, the physical embodiment of things and Agents, with all the variety and specificity that entails, both shapes and limits contract completeness since physical things have a related but separate reality from the symbols of words and numbers.

On this last point one typically thinks of the defects and limitations of natural language, that is, verbal communication, both oral and written. But it should be kept in mind that mathematical language is no less incomplete, just in a different way. This is why words are often used in contracts, to cover 'fuzzy' situations and future things that cannot be specified exactly during the writing of the agreement and which mathematics is too 'tight' to encompass. Whatever language is employed, it will be incomplete and thus so will be the contract.

Property rights are a core component of contracts and of the market economy generally. The rights to use a good or service must be established and the real-world embodiment of things presents issues that earlier theories did not adequately consider. Coase (1937) not only theorised about the economic basis of the firm but he famously introduced property rights into the economic equation. He argued that so long as a property right was established for something, it did not matter who had that right to guarantee that an efficient contract, taking transactions costs into account, would be arrived at through private negotiations in the service of mutual gain. His was an argument against government regulation beyond property right definition and assignment. The field of Law and Economics came into being as a result of this argument.

Coase laid out his case in the context of harms (or 'torts' to use the legal term) and liability for that harm. The traditional solution for many torts was government prohibition, as for example banning a paper plant from dumping effluent into a river. Coase claimed that all one had to do was either give the plant the right to dump effluent or the residents along the river the right to a clean waterway to achieve an outcome that was more efficient than a fiat by the state. Once a right was set either way each party would have an incentive to negotiate with each other and arrive at an outcome that maximised utility by minimising transactions costs.

Coase was not focused on fairness: if the plant had the right to pollute, it gains at the expense of river users and vice-versa. Efficiency was his concern. If one party had lower transactions costs than another then there would be a preferred property right assignment. The party with lower costs of negotiating should receive the right since this was the lower cost way to an optimum.

However, all of this 'Coasean' logic is implicitly disembodied. Despite Coase's own use of the homespun example of sparks from a railway causing fire damage to farmer crops and going through the dynamics of what would happen if the right to set fire was assigned to the railroad versus the right to undamaged crops assigned to the farmer, an exposition that established a whole tradition of such themes in the Law and Economics literature, in fact one could as easily speak of widget damage coming from putty-clay capital machines. The damages and benefits are entirely abstract and the calculations can be done without reference to any real physical world. This is consistent with the disembodied capital and labour and purely mathematical production and utility functions that are the staples of neoclassical market transactions.

For many purposes this is a fine approximation – but not always. Interestingly, almost anticipating some of the behavioural economics literature, the physical realities of some transactions need to be accounted for, even in the largely neoclassical frame. These situations create some unique theoretical contracting problems.

In particular, many assets are in fact relationship-specific in which the value or return on an asset is based on and moulded by the specific parties who have invested in it. This can lead to a variety of less than perfectly competitive results, especially 'quasi-rents' from asset specificity, which is the economic term for the ability to squeeze extra-normal returns above marginal cost from users by asset owners who have a sort of monopoly power. From a contractual point of view, this means that one party can 'hold up' the other to extract those quasi-rents and things like trust between parties now become important intangibles in deciding who to work with and how to work with them and also in writing up and enforcing contracts between parties.

Oliver Williamson (1985: 12), firmly in the neoclassical camp, calls the creation of relationship specific assets the 'fundamental transformation' because this is when 'large number' dynamics of market transactions are converted to 'small number' negotiations between two or few players. Such situations in the neoclassical mode lead to Game Theory situations. Game Theory aims to model the realm of actor behaviour in which forces turn from impersonal (many buyers and sellers trading in identical goods and services with outcomes being driven by statistical forces of collective market dynamics) to personal (few buyers and sellers whose choices and actions inter-depend on the personality and motives and decisions of the negotiators and which are hard to predict based on purely probabilistic reasoning, something game theorists call 'strategic behaviour'). The term suggests 'strategy' and in business, strategy is often paramount, as not everything is impersonal in nature in the business world or the world of the corporation.

The neoclassical paradigm recognises and incorporates this wrinkle in the following way. Technical efficiency is defined as maximum output yielded from minimum inputs (the focus solely on the technical and material transformation of raw inputs into final products and services for sale, anywhere along the production chain); economic efficiency is the maximum benefit yielded from minimum cost (the physical outputs and inputs now monetised using market prices and the optimum incorporating not just technical efficiency but maximum welfare in the market); and agency efficiency – the critical governance aspect – refers to the minimising of transaction, coordination and agency costs, all of which arise from TCE and the Agency Problem that create the internal markets of the firm in the first place.

Oliver Williamson (1983, 1985) calls the balancing of these three efficiency levels across a vertically integrated firm 'economising'. This process consists of deciding on the optimal mix of arms-length transactions undertaken through the market and internal transactions conducted within the firm. There does seem to be an implicit assumption here though that market transactions are largely disembodied while internal ones are embodied and thus subject to more human complexity. File this for the moment: it will arise again in the behavioural economics realm.

One way to think of things thus far is that economic forces generally govern transactions outside firms, while governance represents the means by which nonmarket transactions are managed within firms. Key tasks for the firm are to: (1) pick the right level of integration across activities, essentially an organisational architecture design choice; and then (2) provide efficient governance across that level of integration, which basically amounts to implicit and explicit contract (read: incentive) design.

Task (1) is essentially outside the scope of this conversation, though it cannot be excluded entirely and has been addressed somewhat in the discussion of organisational architecture. Task (2), the core one, can be boiled down largely to contract design. Jensen and Meckling (1979) and Alchian and Demsetz (1972) have written the key articles in this regard. Jensen and Meckling argue that agency contracts involve writing terms that align Principal and Agent utility functions. This process involves agency costs of three types.

1   Monitoring costs, expended by the Principal, to monitor the Agent's behaviour. Such costs can be shifted to the Agent, at least partially, through lower remuneration to poorly performing ones (lowered Agent remuneration to account for lower performance is referred to as 'price protection'). For example, management fees can be lowered for bad management and bad credit risks will pay higher interest in the case of borrowing/lending transactions.

2   Bonding costs, which refer to actions taken by Agents to avoid or limit price protection, e.g. providing quarterly management reports to Principals. The idea here is that Agents have some incentive to report on themselves so as to reassure Principals that they have nothing to worry about. Obviously a rational self-interested maximiser is going to freely provide information only up to the point where the marginal benefits of lowered levels of price protection equal the marginal direct and indirect costs of providing that information.

3   Residual costs, which refer to the 'deadweight' loss of welfare incurred from the ultimate inability to perfectly align Principal/Agent utility functions. This is analogous to the 'welfare triangles' of Tax Theory in which the imposition of a tax by government drives a 'wedge' between the price paid by consumers and the price received by producers. In the tax case the government does receive tax revenue but, except in exceptional circumstances, this transfer of resources to the government is less than the welfare (utility) loss to consumers and producers sacrificed through the tax because those consumers and producers are each paying after-tax prices which do not equal the Marginal Cost (MC) of production or the Marginal Utility (MU) of the consumer. This violates the P=MC condition of perfectly competitive equilibrium and the Pareto optimum it is supposed to bring. In the tax case this welfare loss is justified only if the government provides benefits through its spending greater than that loss. In the governance case this agency loss, to coin a term, is justified only if the benefits of the governance structure outweighs its costs.

In general, within the firm Principals and Agents are both paying different after-agency cost prices and so a 'first-best' equilibrium (which yields a Pareto optimum) is not obtained because none of the respective prices are equal to marginal cost and hence to one another. Since Agent and Principal internal prices (incentives) are not equal to their respective marginal costs and benefits within the firm, the result is residual Agent Opportunism as they seek to get as much as they reasonably can from the Principal, without killing their Golden Goose, so to speak.

Fama (1980) ties all this to different forms of the Efficient Market Hypothesis (EMH) which is the financial market equivalent of perfect neoclassical competition in the economic goods and services markets. The so-called strong form of the EMH posits an inability to make consistent extra-normal profits from financial market transactions because all information is complete and available to everyone and financial markets are perfectly competitive. Less strong forms of the EMH, especially those with information asymmetries, yield more residual loss from Agent Opportunism, as well as more systematic biases in financial security prices.

These generalities have specific manifestations in particular governance and market settings. So there is a general Principal–Agent Problem, but not all Principals and Agents are alike. There are 'classes' of Principal and Agents, e.g. shareholders and managers, or suppliers and producers, or borrowers and lenders, and managers and employees. The Agency problem arises in all these settings and they sometimes have different quirks. Contracts, explicit and implicit, that are entirely internal to the firm are designed to address a general problem. That conceptual task is therefore simple. The devil is in the details of specific contracts for specific Principals and Agents in specific contexts.

For a firm the key Principal is the owner that supplies the capital. So the first type of contract to consider is that which determines the terms of relationship between the owner and her Agent, i.e. the firm manager. The instrument for spelling this out is the management contract. Immediately it is clear that the less ownership the manager has in the firm the greater the potential difference in Principal/Agent incentives and the greater the agency problem might be.

The firm can more broadly be seen as a focal point in the market for contracting between many parties, a sort of centre of an economic nexus (Jensen and Meckling 1979). Parties to this nexus include not only owners and managers, but employees, suppliers, labour unions, stock and bondholders, banks, insurers and customers (Hart 2009). Contracts in this case can be external to the firm as well as internal to it, depending upon how the firm and its relationships are organised, and whether the firm and external parties contracts are mediated through the market, at least in part. This external bargaining is one part of the governance task, if indeed it is applicable. It is not always; if, for example, there are many parties to the nexus (such as customers) and the presence of strong market competitive pressures impinging on and penetrating into the firm, the market mechanism can work its magic without much explicit or implicit contracting.

These are the problems to be grappled with. Let's step back a bit and consider a few standard prescriptions for 'optimal' contracting which theory suggests will ameliorate the Principal–Agent conundrum. The most basic one is how corporate Principals, who own the firm and put capital at risk into it, deal with

Agents they hire to manage the overall enterprise. In this simplest formulation one can imagine two individuals, the Principal (Owner) and the Agent (Manager). Their interests will not be aligned. There are several reasons why according to standard theory and depending upon their extent this affects the design of the optimal contract.

1   Risk aversion. Managers have significant undiversifiable human capital tied up in the firm and so prefer to minimise their risk rather than maximise firm value through highest Net Present Value (NPV) investments.
2   Dividend retention. Managers may prefer to retain earnings in their 'empire' for their own benefit, rather than return it to shareholders who can spend it as they choose.
3   Time horizon. Shareholders have an infinite horizon, managers only the time of their tenure. So even if managers are not seeking to 'game' the situation, they are optimising over a different time frame than owners and the results of their benefit-cost calculations will inevitably differ.

All of these issues lead to the first set of 'standard' types of contract provisions to limit these Principal/Agent wedges. Several typical classes of provisions include the following which deal mostly with relating executive compensation to firm value.

1   Compensate managers in part with shares or options in the company. To at least a degree this should ameliorate all three drivers above by making managers part-owners and thus bringing their time, payout and risk horizons closer in line.
2   Tie manager remuneration to share price or earnings. This extends the incentives above to non-owning managers, or those with a small stake in the firm.
3   Set time horizons of contracts at the just the right length to align Agent motivations with Principal motivations. This obviously is designed to make sure both Principals and Agents are optimising over the same time horizon.

All of these solutions are quite imperfect, as is well known, especially given unreliability in the accounting measures that must be used in contracts and information advantages held by incumbent managers. Also, each one is a partial solution not a total one and sometimes unintended consequences can arise especially where one type of incentive might have complex interactions with another one or some gap is present which cannot or is not adequately covered in contract terms. But these sorts of provisions are clear corporate policy implications of the model which have at their core Principal–Agent alignment issues. The large literature on actual performance of these devices will be considered later in the context of behavioural economics specifically.

The governance issues relating to implicit and explicit contracts between shareholders and debtholders is analogous but not identical (Smith and Warner

1979). This discussion need not detain the reader too long as it is largely external to the firm formally speaking and more direct market pressure can be brought to bear on Agents in many instances. Since debtholders can be said to be contractual suppliers of capital to the firm they can be considered temporary Agents to the shareholders which are the firm's Principals. However, unlike managers and employees, debtholders are external actors who contract through the market, not outside of it. The means of evading Principal oversight look a little different in detail, but the issues are quite parallel to those present in management contracts. Some of these means include the following:

1   Excessive dividend payments as debtholders fear, in extremis, shareholders sucking out firm value, then hiding behind the shield of limited liability.
2   Asset substitution in which managers may overlever their assets to provide shareholders high return and allowing for the fact that shareholders can diversify with limited liability while debtholders get stuck if things go wrong: in other words managers may try to use debt to funnel benefit to shareholders, their primary employer, and away from debtholders.
3   Underinvestment risk, which occurs when shareholders play it safe in situations when they see return on risky investments going to debt-holders not owners. In a sense this is the reverse of asset substitution when a levered firm will only choose to invest in projects that pay off all debt and not just some debt since debtors have priority claim. In this case it is owners who are seeking to extract benefit from their lenders and not managers who in the above scenario are a go-between.
4   Claim dilution, which occurs when the firm issues debt of higher priority than that already on issue, thus diluting existing debtholders. Here debtholders are being played off one another by shareholders or their managers.

In the realm of corporate finance governance, if one can use that term, the remedies are mostly of the formal legal sort, external in nature, and widely practiced and accepted. Principals are generally price protected through bond covenants such as restricting production and investment uses of bond proceeds (which addresses issues 2 and 3); putting limits on dividend policy, e.g. limiting payout ratios (this explicitly deals with issue 1); restraining leverage as measured through total bond issuance of corporate debt ratios, etc.; and requiring provision of certain information to lenders and debtholders.

Of course as these are market transactions as well as contractual ones, market dynamics do play a role, sometimes a very great one, in restraining the Agency Problem, which is why that problem is often considered less frequent or severe for firms that get most of their capital from bonding. (There are obviously other risks taken when using leverage, but these are not governance risks.) In very thick and deep financial markets price signals on corporate debt can be very effective in limiting both Principal and Agent malfeasance and opportunism. There is also a very extensive legal knowledge base on writing bond covenants as well as specialised case law and legislation which allows for the writing of more complete contracts.

But there is much scope for uncertainty even here. Agent Opportunism after the fact (ex post, in other words) is assumed to be a problem since Agents, even with good price protection by Principals, will still seek to maximise and work every opportunity as it arises, not all of which may be anticipated when contracts are written. So incentives such as bonuses and penalties must be set up ex post as well as ex ante to deal with inevitable breaches even with strong ex ante contract terms and market constraints. One solution is ex ante efficient contracting which is where Agents may have an incentive of their own to try to cut efficient deals up front with Principals to limit future price protection losses and smooth out their risk. This is accomplished by the Agent through full advance disclosure of their own costs and benefits when negotiating incentives and information provision. This is not guaranteed to happen but it does provide a rational and self-interested basis for self-limiting by Agents in some circumstances (Watts and Zimmerman 1990).

Intuitively both ex post and ex ante efficient contracting can be used but neither is likely to be completely adequate in solving the Agency Problem. Again, the devil-in-the-detail task of contract drafting is left to the practitioner to work out, guided by the theoretical implications which cut both ways and vary according to circumstance.

Let's return, though, to contracting between Principals and Agents that is notionally wholly within the firm. Here there is no direct market pressure, except that which occurs because of the potential for termination of the contract: Owners can go out to market to replace poor performing managers or bad overseers and this does exercise some limit on the agency problem through indirect market pressure. This can be helpful but does not eliminate the problem completely.

Strict neoclassical thought claims no need of assuming different Principal/Agent utility functions but argues wedges arise simply from different abilities to diversify risk away. If this is the case, then some solutions do arise. One solution is to specify and provide as much information as possible in advance, which is analogous to ex ante efficient contracting. It is a bit different of a concept because it merely argues for such advance disclosure rather than arguing that it might happen of its own accord. Holmström (1979) posited the 'informativeness principle', arguing that it is productive to include all performance indicators that provide additional information about employee effort, assuming measures are low cost, because this yields better risk bearing and more efficient effort choice. However, if one includes actor information processing costs as part of transactions costs, then even the neoclassical paradigm recognises a trade-off between amount of information made available and the costs of making sense of it all. In other words, more may not always be better using a broad definition of transactions costs that include limitations on human abilities to analyse data; hence the informativeness principle may need to be qualified.

If we accept, nonetheless, that more measurement is better, and more provision of performance measures and terms and conditions is better, how do we best actually measure performance and how do we provide incentives for good outcomes? Notice that there is usually a disjunct between desired outcomes and measured performance. So a critical governance challenge is the design of performance standards in all the various contracts, ranging from explicit negotiated agreements between two parties, down through formal employee handbooks, and including implicit and informal ways of doing business.

The literature on performance measures is large and cannot be summarised here. But a few general points are in order. The first is whether to use relative versus absolute performance standards. Measuring performance of one Agent relative to others may encourage competition between Agents and limit opportunism. But it can also encourage regression to the mean and provide incentives to lower competitors' performance rather than raise your own. Collusion within the measurement group is also possible, as with workers who employ social and other pressure to keep high performers down at a certain level because it 'spoils it for the rest of us'. Defining appropriate peer groups and reward thresholds is critical to handle managerial or peer collusion to game the standard.

This issue is general across scale, that is, firm level down through individual pay for performance metrics, but there are also some unique aspects at particular scales. At the individual level there is the relationship between a given job and its specific tasks. Some jobs have a narrow relationship to discrete tasks with clear outcomes. Take for example a bike messenger versus a flight attendant, a pharmaceutical sales rep versus a research scientist, and a grape harvester versus a vintner (Besanko et al. 2007, 483). It is easier to measure performance and incentivise actions to yield desired outcomes for the former in each pair than for the latter.

Also perverse incentives arise with more complex jobs, e.g. teacher performance pay based on standardised test performance. These problems can be addressed through monitoring, job design and alternatives to performance pay. But of course these measures can be administratively costly.

Causality is thus a very important consideration. One must make sure ultimately rewarded performance is actually under employee influence and not just randomly affected. Especially for multitask jobs, unrewarded and unmeasured performance is often given short shrift by the person doing the task while measured and rewarded performance is given priority, perhaps unproductively if measures are incomplete or improperly defined. Multicausality needs to be explicitly taken into account in designing performance measures, e.g. sales are generally affected by more than direct Agent actions so sales measures may need to be adjusted for things like macroeconomic or industry business cycle. But mistakes here can have serious consequences for firm efficiency. This particular discussion is with reference to employees but they also apply at the top management level.

Teamwork presents special issues. How does one design incentives to avoid 'free rider' activity in which some team members try to coast off of the efforts of others? One could avoid team efforts altogether, but often teaming is the most productive means of accomplishing a goal. Its cooperative nature however is not easy to fit into the atomistic and competitive neoclassical model. Even without free riding, individual contribution may be hard to identify and incentivise. No single solution exists but smaller teams and those working together for a long time are less prone to free rider issues and team versus individual performance is usually easier to assess and disentangle in those instances. So one way to deal with this is not through contracting but through team composition and design, rather analogous to the broader issue of organisational architecture.

Contracting costs themselves may necessitate incomplete contracts. It may be possible to have all contingencies laid out but too costly to do so practically or to monitor and enforce all the contingencies. Proprietary and privileged information may also limit contract completeness. And, as already mentioned, some contingencies cannot be laid out at all due to limits set by reality such as uncertainty and the unknowns of the future.

Direct administrative control and coordination is one solution to the issues presented thus far and indeed is always an alternative to contracting or, more usually, one employed in tandem with it, to greater or lesser degree. This entails some level of bureaucracy, a necessary but welfare-losing evil by neoclassical lights. Administrative solutions have the surface appeal of being direct and flexible. If there is a 'benevolent dictator' and/or an 'enlightened populace' this can work better than contracting. But as Churchill said of democracy, contracting may be the worst possible system but all others are worse. Then again, most firms are not democracies.

The discussion now rounds back to organisational structure issues. This is generally outside governance discussions per se but the issues are parallel. Scale and scope of the firm tend to suggest potentially preferred modes of organisation. Large vertically integrated firms generally need partitioning, such as divisions, simply to be able to maintain effective oversight and direction. As usual partitioning requires trade-offs of efficiency in one dimension versus another, mainly coordination versus control.

Decision-making itself, strategic and otherwise, can be broken down into parts which entail some specific issues and tradeoffs of their own. Fama and Jensen (1985) say that decision-making can be broken down into initiation (generation of proposals for resource allocation and contract structuring), ratification (choices of decision initiatives to be implemented), implementation (execution), and monitoring (measuring performance and making rewards). Each of these sub-tasks should be considered when structuring a firm and also when designing its governance.

Two broad structural coordination alternatives follow from this component model of decision-making and implementation. They may be used in tandem and are not necessarily mutually exclusive, especially in a large enterprise with multiple layers. These are as follows:

1 Autonomy/self-containment, in which units are autonomous and information flow between units is minimal; one example is profit centres where units are responsible for and controlled on the basis of profit targets or a responsibility centre where the focus is other than profit e.g. cost or revenue.
2 A lateral relationship model where relations across units are formally or informally emphasised, important when close coordination of work across units is key. A matrix organisation is a formalisation of an informal maximum lateral relationship.

Decisions are one thing. Authority to carry out decisions is another. In all of these models the level of authority centralisation must be considered. And this is where the classic typology developed by Williamson (1983) is pertinent. The unitary functional structure or U-form, has single functional departments reporting straight to a central headquarters (HQ). The multidivisional structure or M-form, has autonomous divisions reporting to HQ with departments within divisions. Williamson argues that an M form improves efficiency beyond a certain size by allowing division managers to focus on operational issues and top management to focus on strategic issues. Agency problems are also supposedly reduced because division competition for funds creates an competitive internal capital market. If HQ staff is weak then the M form may devolve into a holding company with less value creation. This indicates that formal organisation and authority can diverge from informal organisation and authority, that is, actual practice on the ground. The dynamics in this template, though, are purely economic.

A matrix structure organises along two or more dimensions at once often with two reports or more for unit employees. This form is especially useful when economies of scale or scope might be gained through strong lateral relationships. The need for simultaneous coordination argues for a matrix. Businesses that rely on sequential coordination could be better handled hierarchically.

A network structure, finally, is one where the worker, usually with specialised and unique human capital, is the fundamental unit of value creation. The diamond retail industry is an example. Sometimes networks can approximate large firms with a so-called virtual corporation. Modular organisations are a form of network in which relatively self-contained subunits are linked through a technology that focuses on standardised linkages.

A wrap-up

To summarise all this, governance can be boiled down a set of organisational architecture design choices in the neoclassical economic model. Owners seeking to maximise value and minimise Principal–Agent conflicts need to consider the following.

1 Assignment of decision rights to Agents within the firm.
2 Methods to incentivise Agents so they act in accordance with the desires of the Principals.
3 Performance measurement and evaluation systems.
4 Control and coordination systems which sit on top of this.

All this is embedded in corporate culture, which in the neoclassical model is seen basically as another web of implicit incentive structures. But the waves of behavioural economics now begin to lap upon the neoclassical island and this is the topic of the next chapter.

3 Behavioural approaches to decision-making and analysis

Behavioural economics: what it is and is not

A lot of time can be spent on defining the boundaries of behavioural economics. Its reliance on empirical observations of human behaviour might lead one to think it is a branch of experimental economics, which uses laboratory and observational methods of induction to form and test theory. Its focus on human actions that seem to deviate from the assumptions of rationality, maximising and optimisation have some common cause with evolutionary economics, a field which borrows from the Darwinian paradigm of progression and survival of a species in which there are temporary twists and turns that might seem non-optimal short-term but which are evolutionarily 'fit' when taking a long view. The very term 'behavioural' conjures up a departure from the mechanistic deductive model of standard economics that evokes an image of a radically human-centred approach to understanding economic phenomena.

In fact the field is actually fairly easily defined. Broadly speaking, it takes the neoclassical paradigm but adjusts it according to current knowledge of human psychology in domains relevant to economic behaviour. A working template for the field seems to capture most of the research approach that is labelled as behavioural. Adapting Camerer and Lowenstein's (2004) framework, behavioural economics generally follows this methodological trajectory.

1   Identify normative assumptions used by most neoclassical economists.
2   Identify clear violations of these as observed in practice (often thus referred to as anomalies).
3   Try to eliminate these anomalies by explaining them in neoclassical terms.
4   If (3) does not work, the anomalies remain and become behavioural assumptions off of which new models can be built.
5   Derive fresh implications from these new models and test them. (Based on text from 2004: 7.)

Put this way the field can clearly be seen to be an incremental adjustment of the neoclassical model rather than a completely new paradigm. In fact that model is defaulted to as if it were a superior alternative to be changed only if necessary.

The essential behavioural economics model

The basic outlines of behavioural economics can be seen in two very influential books about the field: *Nudge*, by Richard Thaler and Cass Sunstein (2009) and *Thinking, Fast and Slow*, by Daniel Kahneman (2011). Kahneman's book is especially notable since he is a psychologist and one who can be said to have given birth to the field of behavioural economics in his work with fellow psychologist, the late Amos Tversky. In fact Kahneman won the Nobel Prize in Economics in 2002 (Tversky would have been awarded it as well but he had died and the prize is given only to living people).

Thaler and Sunstein's book offers a distinction that Kahneman uses and expands upon, that of 'Humans' and 'Econs'. 'Econs' are the neoclassical actors who meet all the standard assumptions and therefore behave as theory predicts. 'Humans' are actual people who, it turns out, do sometimes, perhaps often, deviate from how Econs act, and in often regular and systematic ways.

Why is there a difference between these two types? The basis is the model of human cognition currently in vogue (keeping in mind these models change over time, often radically). Cognitive psychologists currently see the human being as having two 'systems', referred to as 'System 1' and 'System 2', which is the Seussian terminology of academic psychology and the basis for Kahneman's title *Thinking, Fast and Slow*. Thaler and Sunstein borrow this model but instead use the terms 'involuntary' and 'voluntary' attention centres, which Kahneman also uses at times.

System 1 is quick and intuitive, identified with instinct. System 2 is where rational, thoughtful and analytical thinking is centred. System 1 operates effortlessly in familiar situations where habitual and subconscious or unconscious processing is generally effective. System 2 is well suited to complex or unfamiliar situations, and is associated with 'subjective experience of agency, choice, and concentration' (Kahneman 2011, 21). Self-control and willpower are thought to be centred in System 2 and Kahneman characterises it as slow and reflective, hence the 'slow' of his book's title. System 1, with its instinct, impulse and emotion, is generally fast and immediate in response, hence the 'fast' thinking.

'Econs', the archetypal Homo Economicus, basically have only a System 2. System 1 is not particularly useful or relevant in the theoretically disembodied and atomistic world these characters live in. 'Humans' have Systems 1 and 2 because they have to move around and live in this embodied world in which often one needs to act quickly, with incomplete information and in ambiguous situations. Having both systems is well adapted to the real world. But there are times when the 'fast' System 1 leads to systematic deviations from the behavioural predictions of neoclassical Economic Theory. It is from System 1 that most of the anomalies, biases and errors arise. In other words there are situations where System 2 does a better job of making economic decisions but System 1 is what predominates. Thaler and Sunstein and Kahneman are both at pains to point out that System 1 is not 'bad' and in fact it is this system that both makes us human and is uniquely adapted to survival in actual environments, especially more 'primitive' ones.

This model is clearly based on current models of brain structure, which are actually tripartite rather than dual (Glimcher and Fehr 2013; Marshall and Magoun 2013). These posit three layers of brain structure, the innermost being the most 'primitive' and the first to form in humans, and the last being the most recent and hence the most evolutionarily advanced. Although all models must simplify, there are implicit value judgements inherent in those simplifications. In this case there is a standard but unspoken assumption of 'progress' in which 'lower' biology is necessary but beneath the higher functions of reason, thought and deliberation.

Kahneman explicitly notes that the System metaphor is just that, descriptive, not literal, and a way to simplify psychological insights in a way most intelligible to Humans who best understand narratives. This is a significant qualifier for although based on currently available empirical evidence, the actual workings of the brain can only be indirectly observed through things such as neural activity. The human brain is considered to be one of the most complex organisms in the known universe and still highly impenetrable to complete analysis by that same brain. Twenty years from now brain models will almost certainly be quite different than today and even then will likely not be the final word. For this reason, the discussion in this chapter will emphasise broad facts drawn from the mass of empirical observations of what people actually do under certain circumstances and focusing less on the present speculation about why humans are doing what they do, although sometimes this must be addressed to arrive at workable predictions about cause and effect.

The behavioural model also largely ignores the rest of the body, being purely psychological. The brain-centred and cognition-centred nature of behavioural economics is made very clear in Jolls, Sunstein and Thaler (1998) in which they speak of 'bounded rationality', 'bounded willpower' and 'bounded self-interest'. These concepts are carried forward and used in Nudge. It is very revealing that Jolls et al. use as a starting point a quote from Nobel prize winner Gary Becker who is also the archetype of the neoclassical hardline economist: "[A]ll human behavior can be viewed as involving participants who [1] maximize their utility [2] from a stable set of preferences and [3] accumulate an optimal amount of information and other inputs in a variety of markets" (1998: 1476). This is a very limited view of economics much less human behaviour, and can be said to represent a 'strong' neoclassical model. So behavioural economics in this treatment and many others is to put 'bounds' on these rather extreme premises rather than build a new foundation (Jolls et al. 1998)

Considering each 'bound' in turn, bounded rationality is a term made well known by Herbert Simon in 1955 in which he conducted a study of human problem-solving (in this case university students solving math problems) and then compared their approach with the way computer programs solved problems (Simon 1955). Simon found that human beings were short on time, information and cognitive 'processing power' and thus took short cuts in problem solving which he called 'heuristics', a concept taken up later by Kahneman and Tversky. As an example, students might try to solve a problem by picking some plausible solution, checking it, and then working from there to the actual solution or at least as close as they could get to it. This is not how an all-powerful computer would solve a problem but humans are not computers. So while neoclassical theory assumes unbounded cognitive ability and memory, in actual fact human beings have limits in these areas and it is important to understand what these limits are and how they affect decision-making. Although this may sound like a significant departure from neoclassicism, in fact it is very much in keeping with optimisation and a benefit-cost approach to decisions, except that now internal brain processing is one of the many scarce resources to be economised on. (In the technical terms of pure constrained optimisation, bounded rationality makes humans more likely to stop at a local optimum rather than a global optimum.)

'Bounded willpower' appears to be a term original to Jolls et al. It is bit harder to define explicitly but the idea is simple enough: neoclassical man will stick to any decision he makes because he has rationally calculated that it is the optimal choice, while actual human beings will not always be able to stick to a resolve, even one they have calculated is best for them. Econs have unlimited willpower, driven by rationality; Humans have limited willpower which cannot always see rationality through.

'Bounded self-interest' is another term that seems to have been invented by these authors. This concept is the most difficult to fathom. It is said to differ from simple altruism, which economists would say occurs when an actor's utility function includes other actors, such as family members: in other words in cases when an actor's utility is increased both by improvements to one's own welfare and the welfare of others that one cares about. Actions under these circumstances can still be termed as self-interest, just using a broader conception of 'self'.

However a different situation exists in the case of a sense of fairness, which human beings appear to exhibit in abundance. In this case actors may not care about the welfare of particular others but they do care about how people generally are treated and also how their own welfare stacks up as compared to that general group. So this is not just an expanded self-interest that includes a select group of individuals close to one's self but a wider concern about how comparable strangers are treated. Nonetheless most behavioural treatments seem to be potentially collapsible into utility maximisation models in which the treatment of others generally are an individual 'argument' in an individual utility function; thus general losses and gains to groups (rather than specific actors known to an individual) affect the utility of the individual actor. In this sense actors remain 'atomistic' in that they exist independent of others though their decisions will be cognitively and emotionally affected by the welfare of others relative to their own. Interestingly, Nobel Prize winner Amartya Sen has written about these issues in a very different way back in a classic article in 1977, so these issues are not new and Sen's treatment is substantially different from the current behavioural view (Sen 1977).

Summarising to this point, one could broadly say that the neoclassical actor is an unbounded utility maximiser while the behavioural economics actor is a bounded utility maximiser, in which cognitive, perceptual and psychological limits cause decisions that sometimes do not conform with optimality as defined by neoclassical theory. Neoclassical optimality generally remains as the desired reference point and the quest of the behavioural economist is not just to understand deviations from this norm but to suggest devices that human beings will actually respond to in correcting them. Thaler and Sunstein summarise all this in their book by saying that if people could pay full attention, possess complete information, have unlimited cognitive abilities and complete self-control then they would make better (optimal) decisions. But as they don't possess these, they make poorer decisions at times (2009: 5).

Despite some interesting findings, theoretically the behavioural approach is not a major departure. In fact Jolls et al. argue that behavioural economics may be deemed as superior to neoclassical economics because, unlike the former, it uses 'empirically validated descriptions of actual behaviour' while retaining most of the supposed 'parsimony' and predictive tightness of the Homo Economicus template (1998: 1489). In other words, this is still the Economic Man model but modified in certain ways that match limited observations of human behaviours in limited domains.

Laissez faire and implicit utilitarian (or consequentalist) value systems dominate, as they do in standard economics, albeit in adjusted form. For this reason, Thaler and Sunstein prefer public policy that consists of 'libertarian paternalism' which 'nudges' but does not force Agents into decisions (2009: 5). Camerer prefers 'asymmetric paternalism' which seeks to guide the least sophisticated Agent while giving freer reign to everyone else. 'Consumer sovereignty' and atomism remain fundamental to the worldview and the policy prescriptions, while interesting and even useful, are quite mild, and quite close to the classical 'liberalism' of 19th-century economists and policy-makers. Mild, except to neoclassical economists, who seem to get quite excited over the mildest spice in their usual broth.

Behavioural economics: basic current findings

There is a now a large literature containing a catalogue of findings from behavioural economics. There is quite a bit of repetition in this literature: despite all the pages many of the findings still mirror or repeat Kahneman and Tversky's initial work on heuristics and later work done by Kahneman alone.

Rather than provide yet another catalogue, this section will focus on those findings most pertinent to the neoclassical corporate governance literature and possible amendments that these might suggest. This will form the basis of the template developed in Chapter 5 in which some more concrete applications to corporate governance are put forth.

Given that the neoclassical model is the starting point for this book (of course there are other views) and that this model suggests that the main task of corporate governance is to monitor and manage the Agency problem and to control and coordinate activities internal to the firm to achieve ability to compete within the marketplace, behavioural findings will be classified according to how they show actors to deviate from the premises that actors are: (1) rational; (2) maximising; (3) selfish; and (4) atomistic. Other views will be explored in more detail in Chapters 5 and 6.

Modification 1: Actors are not always or entirely 'rational'

The whole behavioural movement really began with Herbert Simon's term of 'bounded rationality.' Simon's concept was entirely cognitive in nature; people were basically the calculating machines of neoclassical theory and their main decisions had to do with 'problem-solving' in a mathematical arena (games such as chess were also a favoured field of study). What Simon introduced was the notion that decision-making/problem solving takes time and effort (processing power) and even for computers these are not unlimited resources. Hence the term 'bounded'.

This term, as shown earlier, is still being used, and behavioural economics largely follows Simon's original heuristics notion. The field has mainly focused on documenting and expanding the list of heuristics and examining the specific ways in which they affect decisions in domains that go far beyond the limited technical ones studied in the 1950s.

What does behavioural economics suggest about the rationality of human beings? This is actually a difficult question to answer in some ways since rationality is not clearly defined or described in the standard model. Vague terms like 'well-ordered' preferences and 'consistent choices' are bandied about but without clear content in many cases. In a rather circular manner rationality generally seems to refer to behaviour and decision-making that is predicted by the model. If actors deviate from these predictions then they can be said to be irrational or at least non-rational or only partly rational.

This is a rather deficient methodology but in fact this seems to be what most behavioural economists mean. For example, Camerer et al. say that 'people often do not understand and interpret situations as economists normally assume. This might take the form of ignoring features of the situation that economists deem to be relevant (such as base rates when making probability judgements) or, conversely, it might involve people being affected by features that economists assume to be irrelevant (such as superficial differences in how options are described)' (2003: 1230). In other words, they don't behave as the model says they should and it is the predictions of the model itself that define 'rational' behaviour (and optimality as well).

If one accepts this (debatable) starting point, one can then ask two things: (1) in what ways do people observably deviate from the predictions of standard theory; and (2) why do these deviations occur? More time will be spent here on (1) because it has a basis in observations that 'objective' observers can agree upon. (2) does have importance, especially for policy prescriptions since if one wants to change an effect one has to be fairly confident of the causes that must be addressed. But (2) is more problematic. Economists and cognitive psychologists posit a number of mental models to explain why people do what they do, but by no means are these unassailable and at times they are biased towards the original model and premises that economists subscribe to. In fact, it is these premises that must be tested and challenged. One critic thus sees 'behavioural economics not as a challenge to standard economics at all but rather as a friendly amendment: an attempt to rescue it from its growing theoretical and practical difficulties, even though this is not always recognized and appreciated by the discipline's hardliners' (Streeck 2010: 388).

Philosophically there are still some issues to grapple with and only a relatively small part of the current literature really attempts to do so. (There is much larger and older economic methodology literature that has delved into, though not resolved, the notion of rationality; strangely this is mostly ignored by behavioural theorists as of yet.) If actors deviate from neoclassical rationality, one still has to put some structure on the nature of these deviations. The simplest scenario is that actors are rational in the neoclassical sense but that transactions costs of information retrieval, processing and analysis limit their ability to be fully rational in the pure sense: hence, bounded rationality. In other words, people could see reality 'appropriately' if they lived in a pure world but because of physical and cognitive limits cannot always do the full calculations needed to arrive at this.

This raises the question of defining 'full rationality', which, for Camerer, consists of well-defined preferences (or goals), making of decisions to maximise preferences, preferences that accurately reflect the time costs and benefits of available options, well-informed beliefs in situations of uncertainty about how uncertainty will resolve itself, and when, new information becomes available, an update of beliefs according to Bayes' Law, or rule, (Camerer et al. 2003: 1214–1215). This is actually quite consistent with what other leading behavioural writers explicitly posit as an ideal, including Kahneman and Thaler. This is how Homo Economicus is supposed to act. We'll return to the all-important issue of uncertainty which has here been reduced to a rather deterministic footnote but for now take it for granted that it can be modelled fully enough to be prone to a reasonable benefit–cost analysis.

Two nuances arise at this point. The first surrounds the nature of optimisation and the second surrounds the mechanics of bounded rationality, that is how it actually operates, how constraining it actually is and whether some areas of decision-making are more prone to it than others.

On optimisation, Smith (2007), following Hayek (1945), contrasts the 'constructivist rationality' of neoclassical economics with 'ecological rationality' which tends to produce good outcomes in practice regardless of whether its workings conform to Social Science Theory. Some apparently irrational patterns of individual preference might be better understood as components of ecologically well-adapted institutions (1945: 559). And, indeed, this is the stuff of evolutionary economics which focuses on longer-term adaptation rather than short-term and repeated optimisation (McQuillen and Sugen 2012). Indeed, some authors claim that bounded rationality may be globally rational if it truly economises scarce cognitive processing time and energy as well as everything else. It is only 'irrational' if it results from the 'errors' of heuristics or other biases (Korobkin and Ulen 2000: 1076). Melvin Eisenberg is quoted by one such author by saying that the difference may often be between searching for the sharpest needle in the haystack and searching for a needle sharp enough for sewing (2000: 1078). In many cases it makes more sense to stop at the sharp enough needle. Of course this kind of reasoning can be dangerously tautological, as indeed a good deal of sociobiology can be.

To summarise, optimality as a concept largely remains based on a mechanistic and technical idea. 'Beginning in 1960 cognitive psychology become dominated by the metaphor of the brain as an information-processing device replacing the behaviourist conception of the brain as a stimulus-response machine. The information processing metaphor permitted a fresh study of neglected topics like memory, problem solving and decision-making' (Camerer and Loewenstein 2004: 6). This is a very limiting way of putting things and in many ways it is the metaphor of a computer that determines the analogies, e.g. 'problem-solving' and 'processing'. But it does have the advantage of being simple (perhaps simplistic), allowing one to use the neoclassical predictions with relatively little modification, including that of optimisation.

Not explored in any detail in most of the behavioural economics literature is the actual procedure of decision making. (The psychology literature obviously studies this in detail and some of this is brought into Kahneman's work.) The economics focus is mostly on the incorporation of psychological elements in the utility function, without interrogating that function's existence. There are some exceptions, such as Selten (1998) who proposes three levels of reasoning and Rubinstein (1988) who follows Tversky's work on a procedure called similarity which refers to ways in which preferences might be constructed by actors. These types of approaches often move away from utility maximisation entirely and require considerable new theory building. The economic methodology literature has a long history of alternative ideas, as does psychology, but this foundation remains largely ignored at present (Rubinstein 2007: 1244).

Even keeping within utility maximisation parameters presents a wide range of possible models of rationality. Rubinstein (2007) distinguishes between actions as: (1) Cognitive: an action which involves a reasoning process; (2) Instinctive: an action which involves instinct; or (3) Reasonless: an action likely to be the outcome of a random process with little or no reasoning about the decision problem. Korobkin and Ulen (2000: 1060–1061) posit a spectrum from 'thin' Rational Choice Theory ranging from 'thick' down to 'thin', where thin versions are relatively undemanding and are consistent with a wide range of behaviours and thick conceptions have more robust behavioural predictions more easily falsifiable. The range of thin through thick ranges from the expected utility model (discussed later) to a self-interest version and through to a wealth maximising version. One can see that neoclassical rationality is closely tied to degrees of optimisation since the fact of optimal behaviour (however defined) is said to be prima facie proof of rational choice while its absence suggests a 'failure' of some sort.

Bounded rationality generally is a concept that might conceal as much is it reveals. Perhaps bounded cognition would be a better phrase since really all that is usually suggested is a limitation on memory, storage and processing power with an implicitly computer-based calculation process going on in the foreground.

Human beings, however, are more complex than machines, and human 'rationality' may need a different model than the one currently used. There are references to this in the behavioural literature, to be sure, though they have not yet led to a new model, even a hybrid one. One example is cognitive ease: good mood, clear display of information and related experience all lead to a feeling of familiarity, truth, goodness, and ease of effort when human beings face challenges. Kahneman notes that if you feel strained you will likely work harder, be vigilant and suspicious, feel less comfortable and make fewer errors but also be less intuitive and less creative (2011: 60) Exposure to something, even briefly, breeds familiarity which then can cause us to be biased, or imagine we know something (e.g. whether someone is a celebrity) even when we don't. Presentation, e.g. clear or bold fonts or certain colours, also bias us if they are cognitively easy for us. Interestingly, one experiment showed that fewer errors were made on a word problem when the font was harder as opposed to easier to read (2011: 65). These are all things obviously inapplicable to a computer.

So while bounded rationality as typically defined is pretty simple, actual field observations reveal some odd effects, typically human. Some interesting illusions arise from distinctly human cognitive and energetic limits. Chabris and Simon note 'the invisible gorilla', for instance, in which half of people concentrating on counting the number of passes made by members of a white uniformed team to a black uniformed one did not notice the presence of a person in a gorilla costume walking in halfway through on the screen for 9 seconds (Kahneman 2011). An analogous example is the finding of one study that radiologists contradict their own diagnosis of x-rays 20% of the time looking at the same picture, even within a few minutes. Similar results are found in other professions (2011: 225).

In essence, self-control and cognitive effort are forms of mental work and not only is there only so much effort to go around but humans are affected by that work in very particular ways. 'Ego depletion' is the term coined by Roy Baumeister who has shown that, for example, if you force yourself to do something you do more poorly later on other tasks that require mental effort, like cognition. And it is not just metaphorical. He found that the nervous system consumed more glucose when mentally effortful tasks were undertaken. What this implies and what observations show is that tired people make poorer decisions and decisions are affected by glucose levels which fluctuate throughout the day. So some time periods, e.g. after lunch, are bad times to schedule decisions. And decision-makers should be properly fed since restoration of glucose levels improves performance (Kahneman 2011: 44–45).

This, of course, is where Kahneman and Tversky's (and Simon's) 'heuristics' come in, characterising the short cuts that Humans are said to use to deal with actual situations using the processes and resources that nature has given them. Heuristics is simply a conceptualisation of what is going on inside the actor and not the same thing as the real behaviour or process.

Still, there has been an impressive compilation of observations of how humans actually seem to behave under certain conditions in which relevant information is available and a choice set is clearly presented but in which they deviate from the way neoclassical economists predict they would behave or seem to ignore or misinterpret clearly relevant information. Terms used in the literature are used here, although these terms themselves, such as 'bias', import psychological assumptions into the discussion that a more neutral term would not. Nonetheless, these phenomenon do suggest that human beings often deviate from what a purely deductive logic would suggest.

Here is a list of consistently observed deviations of human actors from standard working definitions of rationality.

The 'present bias' and the 'peanuts effect'. Decision-makers often put heavier weight on costs and benefits that are immediate and less on those that are delayed, even if the delayed effects are equal to or greater than the present ones. In a related manner, people tend to pay less attention to small but cumulative consequences of repeated decisions, e.g. the effect on weight of repeated consumption of sugared beverages or the cumulative health effects of smoking (Loewenstein et al. 2012: 1).

'Anchoring'. This is a phenomenon in which judgement is heavily skewed by contextual information ('anchors') even when that information is clearly random and irrelevant. This effect is strong, measurable and consistent across different levels of expertise by actors exposed to the anchors. Kahneman claims that anchoring sometimes occurs due to insufficient adjustment by people from a starting point, e.g. estimating two inches will differ if you do it from the top of the page or from the bottom up. Mitigating anchoring is a key task of the 'choice architect', to use Thaler and Sunstein's term. One way to do this is to explicitly negate or remove the anchor by changing the context; for example, when negotiating responding to an offer not with a counteroffer but with reasons the offer is not reasonable (Kahneman 2011: 119–126).

There are many examples of anchoring. One example can be found in a study that showed that a sign that says 'Limit 12 per customer' caused people to buy more, anchoring off of the 'limit' of 12 (De Meza et al. 2008: 63–64). Much of the literature focuses on how presentation of information causes people to make wrong estimates of probabilities or quantities, as in the case of a study where students were asked to estimate a figure and were given a US Social Security number as a reference point. Their estimates were very close to the number they were given even though a Social Security number was an arbitrary anchor. Kahneman and Tversky's original work on heuristics included an experiment that gave people a sequence of numbers and asked them to guess what the total was. Estimates were much larger when the sequence began as 9 + 8 + 7 ... as opposed to 1 + 2 + 3 ...

'Framing effects'. Related to anchoring is framing in which the way a choice is framed or presented will change an actor's assessment or decision, even though the actual details of the set of options are unaltered, just expressed differently. For example, a person will almost always pay more for accessories for a suit if the suit is bought first than the other way around. The large purchase may desensitise the person to large outlays and small outlays seem smaller than they are, and consumers pay less attention to making them. (This particular example also could be said to include an anchoring effect as well.) With warranties on financial products, such as mortgage insurance, these are more easily accepted once the larger product (a house or a portfolio) is bought. In a similar vein, investors react differently according to whether long-run results or short-run results are presented (Tapia and Yermo 2007: 8). As can be seen the framing effects can lead to inconsistent choices from a substantively identical choice set, something which is clearly a violation of neoclassical rationality (De Meza et al. 2008: 21).

The 'overconfidence bias' and the 'curse of knowledge'. The overconfidence bias refers to people's tendency to be overconfident in their predictive and assessment abilities. This is especially a problem with 'experts' who think they know more than they actually do. Camerer, Loewenstein and Weber (1989) talk about this bias in the context of the 'curse of knowledge'. Education, for example, may cause people to become overconfident believing they are 'educated' and reinforcing the confirmatory bias that causes people to downplay conflicting evidence. The 'curse of knowledge' specifically refers to the phenomenon of well-informed people often being unable to reproduce the sometimes more accurate judgements of less-informed people (2008: 51). A meta-analysis by Grove et al. (2000) showed that experts did worse than simple statistical methods in making predictions in a criminology domain (De Meza et al. 2008: 52). Overconfidence is obviously a big issue, driven both by the illusion of knowledge and the illusion of control over circumstances (the two often being related) (Tapia and Yermo 2007).

'Completeness bias'. This is a situation where people tend to stop searching too early for an answer if they have generated a hypothesis to answer an open question. This could be related to the overconfidence bias and also to anchoring (De Meza et al. 2008: 67).

The 'planning fallacy'. People underestimate costs and time for completion of projects, something Kahneman chalks up to failure to consult experience from similar undertakings and instead relying on attachments to vivid particulars rather than dry generalities, even if those generalities are known to be true (Kahneman 2011: 249–250).

'Unrealistic optimism' ('Optimism bias'). This involves people's tendency to claim that they are less likely than their peers to suffer harm (De Meza et al. 2008: 60). Behavioural psychologists speculate that this could be caused in part by the law of small numbers, in which people draw too strong inferences from too little information (2008: 50) It also could be caused by cognitive limits on processing or systematic mistakes in inferences about probabilities (a point discussed in more detail below) (2008: 51).

'Choice/information overload'. It is generally assumed that better (more) information improves decisions. But given cognitive limits, more information may deflect attention from what is really important. This leads to a paradox whereby additional accurate information may lead to worse outcomes. For example one study showed that rewriting mortgage disclosure forms designed to reveal broker compensation led to more rather than less confusion (De Meza et al. 2008).

Perhaps for similar reasons, more choice is not necessarily experienced as better by people but simply more demanding and confusing. People offered a small number (six) of chocolates, versus a large number (thirty) were more satisfied with the chocolate they chose and more likely to choose it again during another round. Similar results were found using a similar experiment with a jam display (De Meza et al. 2008). As another example, traditional economics suggests more choice of electrical utilities and plans is better. But behavioural economics suggests that more choice allows more room for mistakes and poorer decisions (including remaining with incumbent suppliers by default) because of information overload (Pollitt and Shaorshadze 2011: 13).

'Hindsight' and 'outcome biases' and the 'halo effect'. These are clustered here because of their close relationship to one another. Hindsight bias refers to how people adjust up their estimates of the knowability or predictability of an event after it occurs. For example, after the Global Financial Crisis many more people 'knew' it would happen than actually did before.

This is related to the 'outcome bias' in which people adjust their stories according to a known outcome, e.g. a CEO becomes a 'winner' after the firm's share price goes up, whereas she may have been described as a 'loser' before then.

These two biases combine with the 'halo effect', in which a generalisation is made about a person or situation based on one particularly vivid characteristic, to create what Kahneman calls a narrative fallacy, i.e. a story to fit the facts that maximises perceived foreknowledge and minimises the role of luck. Conspiracy theories and business management success formulas thrive on this effect (Kahneman 2011: 199–208).

'Self-serving bias', 'belief bias' and 'confirmation bias/myside bias'. Once more these are treated as a cluster. The self-serving bias is the human tendency to attribute positive events to one's own personal character and attribute negative events to external factors. Thus the essence of the old saying that success has a hundred fathers (or mothers) but failure is an orphan. An example would be where an athlete attributes winning a competition to her own efforts and competence but losing one to poor coaching (Mezulis et al. 2004).

The 'belief bias' refers to the situation where people have difficulty evaluating conclusions that conflict with what they think they know about the world (De Meza et al. 2008: 67). Closely related is the 'confirmation bias' or 'myside bias' which refers to the tendency of people to test propositions and generate and weigh evidence in a way consistent with their prior held beliefs (2008: 67).

'Salience'. Many of the effects described thus far are closely related to 'salience' in which a particular stimulus is more noticeable than others around it cognitively or perceptually and hence is given more weight than it deserves on a substantive basis. For example high electricity bills are salient and thus raise vociferous opposition perhaps outweighing incentive effects to reduce consumption in some cases (Pollitt and Shaorshadze 2011: 9). Psychologists speak of 'cue competition' in which more salient cues dominate less salient ones and irrelevant cues make people use more relevant ones less (De Meza et al. 2008). There are many examples of this. One of many can be found in electronic tolling, where one researcher has found that people strongly underestimate what they pay in tolls when these are collected electronically and automatically through systems such as EZPass. This occurs because payments are not salient and thus not noticed (Finkelstein, 2007).

Feedback effects. In many settings clear, immediate and salient feedback is both critical to and has an effect on behaviour (contrary to neoclassical reasoning which suggests that people, given all the facts, will optimise accordingly without being affected by the type or timing of feedback). For example, the US electric utility Southern California Edison gives consumers an Ambient Orb that glows red with high energy use, green with low use and which has been shown to have significant effects on energy usage as opposed to information provided in bills at regular, but not immediate, intervals (Thaler and Sunstein 2009: 190). In another study one set of households received a difficult energy use reduction goal (20%) while another had an easy goal (2%) and some of each group received feedback while the other part did not. Only the households that had the difficult goal and received feedback achieved significant reductions (Pollitt and Shaorshadze 2011: 10–11).

Contextual effects. A major finding of cognitive psychology is how context-dependent thinking and problem-solving can be, including such seemingly straightforward tasks as learning comprehension. For example, in experimental settings, such as formal game playing, subjects may appear to have low intelligence in zero context (or highly abstract) settings, but exhibit much higher functioning when some context is provided, or they make very different choices (Loewenstein 1999: F30). Even simple things like calling a Prisoner's Dilemma game the 'Wall Street Game' versus the 'Community Game' causes dramatically different outcomes (1999: F31). One study in a real world domain found that energy use was more highly impacted by the text of a letter giving energy conservation advice when that letter was on the letterhead from a local energy commission rather than the local utility (Pollitt and Shaorshadze 2011: 12).

An interesting example of contextual effects can be seen in a study that demonstrated that emoticons can have an influence on behaviour. This study showed that people's energy consumption was affected by using the appropriate emoticon. The smiley face ':)' caused people already using less energy than the average to reinforce that behaviour while those using more than the average restrained themselves when given the frowning emoticon ':(' on their respective bills (though the effect was small) (Thaler and Sunstein 2009: 70).

'Regression to the mean'. Regression to the mean refers to the statistical tendency of random effects to cause deviations around a mean in which nonetheless the tendency is toward that mean. So good performance at something (such as a sport) is typically followed by bad and vice versa. In a psychological context Kahneman (2011) points out that human beings have a sharp tendency to attribute a causal story to such random effects and thus make perverse choices or interpretations as a result (2011: 173–184). An example is the well-known belief in 'hot hands' in poker and other games, whereas in most cases evidence shows such sequences to be simply random.

'Less is more fallacy'. This refers to a case where a comparison of alternatives comes out differently depending on whether the comparison is made jointly or separately. For example, one study found that people were willing to pay more for two sets of dinnerware when the two were offered jointly and where one set had pieces with a few broken than when the combined set was instead broken up into two and offered singly, in which case the set with broken pieces was discounted (Kahneman 2011: 160–161). This occurred because the broken pieces were seen by people as less valuable even if the set they were part of had more whole pieces, and the same core of identical ones, than the set without broken pieces (2011). Clearly framing effects may be operating in this case.

Mood-altered judgement. The evidence shows that good moods increase optimism, bad moods increase pessimism and hence there is potential for biases in judgement caused by mood. A specific manifestation is 'projection bias' in which people overestimate how long moods will last, exacerbating the judgement problem (De Meza et al. 2008): Kahneman (2011: 139) asserts that the question 'how do I feel about x' is simpler for most people than 'what do I think about x' and thus people will tend to make decisions based on how they feel more than on what they think. The overall point is that emotion or emotional impairment can affect decision-making, especially if the emotion is not 'appropriate' to the cognition, either in tone (e.g. feeling scared about something that should be positive) or degree (e.g. getting manic rather than just happy). (It should be noted that this statement does betray a preference away from emotional processing and towards purely cognitive processing.)

'Omission/commission bias.' Ilana Ritoy and Jonathan Baron coined this term which refers to the human tendency to care more about errors of commission rather than errors of omission. This could be driven by the desire to avoid the highly unpleasant feeling of regret. Regret is triggered more by occurrences brought about by one's own actions than by outcomes that occur as a result of external forces. This can cause people to avoid actions or situations that may result in a regrettable outcome, or perhaps cause them to reinterpret situations accordingly (Camerer et al 2003: 1224–1225).

Pattern-seeking. Psychologists (and most self-observing people) know well that human beings are pattern seekers. (Existentialist psychologist and Holocaust survivor Victor Frankl would say meaning seekers – see Frankl 2006.) Thus chance events are typically seen as being part of something larger and even experienced statisticians who know the role of randomness in events nonetheless systematically err towards causal inference, especially with small samples where extremes are more prominent and where patterns jump out more. Thus people make up stories based on patterns and become very attached to their stories (Kahneman 2011: 109–118).

This characteristic of the human mind can be clearly seen as the foundation of many of the effects above. The halo effect, already mentioned, is a good example. Recall that this is the phenomenon where that first or isolated impression of someone or something biases observers to assume that this impression applies to the whole person or situation. Kahneman (2011: 85) refers to WYSIATI – 'what you see is all there is' – in which people make up stories based on what they see and assume away the gaps. Pattern-seeking and causal thinking is a big reason why context is so important and a basis for how framing and salience operate.

Many biases interact here. For example given names of two people each with the same six attributes, the person whose list starts with the good attributes is judged more favourably than that with the bad (2011: 82). People given both sides of a legal case are less biased than those given one side, even when both have identical facts (86–87). And labels, e.g. '90% fat free' vs. '10% fat', affect judgements. This is the reason that Kahneman suggests 'decorrelating' errors, for example in meetings having people write out their opinions first before meeting when first or strong opinions are likely to dominate.

There appears to be an interesting structure to human pattern-seeking. Kahneman argues that humans have automatic 'basic assessments' such as attractiveness, that occur whether we want them to or not. Further he indicates that we can form immediate and correct impressions of groups of objects, precisely for four or less, but more crudely for greater numbers, and that we are pretty good at broad relationships, e.g. whether lines are parallel or not. But we must be much more deliberate for things like additive relationships and in those cases use much more cognitive effort as a result which, as already discussed, leads to its own biases. For example people's willingness to donate to an environmental investment did not increase nearly as much as the benefit suggested for different scenarios. For an investment that would save 2,000, 20,000, and 200,000 birds respectively there was not a proportionate increase in willingness to pay which, Kahneman argues, demonstrates that our automatic system has difficulty with quantity (Kahneman 2011: 93).

Pattern-seeking is based on the human mind's associational capacity which is automatic. Shown two words in succession ('bananas' and 'vomit'; Kahneman 2011: 50), one cannot help creating a story and attendant bodily reaction. Kahneman does say (2011: 51) that neuroscience recognises the embodied nature of cognition, i.e. that you think with your body and not just your brain, which is a relatively rare point in the behavioural literature. Associational processes are thus not just based on ideas but also on physical characteristics and context. For example young people who are told to walk slowly are much more likely to associate words with old age than those who are not. People who are shown money cues, e.g. a screen saver with bills floating on water, are more likely to do tasks alone, be more competitive and less likely to help others in staged experimental situations (e.g. picking up dropped pencils) (Kahneman 2011: 55).

'Normalisation', whereby a novel event is incorporated into one's model of everyday reality is, Kahneman argues, an associational process. When we see things repeated in context – e.g. an incident occurring at a particular place more than once, we associate them and see them as 'normal' and then assume a causality (2011: 70–78). Kahneman gives an example from his own experience where he and his wife bumped into a colleague at two different times in two different foreign locations and the second time was less surprised because 'this is now the colleague who I bump into overseas'. Although this particular example, as a couple of others in Kahneman's *Thinking, Fast and Slow* (2011), may sometimes suggest his particular quirks more than a more broad characteristics of human beings in general.

A summing up of rationality biases. The human brain is structured in a very particular way, very well-adapted for some situations (perhaps most that matter in daily life) but limited in others. The general tendency of much of the behavioural literature written by economists and lawyers sometimes gives a more sweeping impression, especially in the use of terms such as 'bounded' which suggest that 'Econs' are what 'Humans' should strive toward, or be nudged toward if need be. Kahneman does exhibit some pre-judgements of his own, though his psychological model is definitely more nuanced. As one can see from this very long list, human beings have been observed to be pretty subtle and complex creatures. Most readers will probably nod in recognition in going through this panoply, probably in a way that they would not do when reading about the calculating machine of Homo Economicus.

These traits would appear to add up to far more than just mere 'boundedness' of rationality in problem solving. Simon, who invented the concept, explicitly was studying the very narrow domain of how students went about solving maths problems. His concept of 'heuristics', or shortcuts, was quite apt there. When applied to all the varied situations of living, however, the approaches that human beings use to make sense of things and formulate and execute decisions are far more than just a collection of shortcuts (though some are indeed that). Rather they make up a mode of existence very specific to the species which has a way of life and being. The continued use of the terms 'heuristics', 'biases' and 'errors' perhaps should be re-thought.

An aside on uncertainty

The bulk of daily life has a certain routine and repetitive nature to it. Picking a meal for breakfast, deciding what amount to tip a waitress, and deciding whether to accept a job offer vary in their frequency, but each has varying degrees of regularity and can be captured by relatively simple conceptual structures. In other words, they can be posited as economic problems in formal terms and a relatively straightforward optimal solution can be arrived at on those terms using the assumptions of neoclassical economics, even with psychological bounds introduced. Thus there are times when more really can be had for nothing if a problem is properly understood and Homo Economicus may have the best set of tools in its limited psychological toolkit. In this case 'nudges' and other means to push Humans towards Econs are appropriate.

However the bounds of reality are much larger than this limited domain. Dealing with uncertainty is one area that is often out of these bounds. The economist Frank Knight famously wrote about the distinction between 'risk' and 'uncertainty' almost one hundred years ago and non-economists have studied it for even longer (Knight 1921). Risk, roughly speaking, can be said tô cover situations where actors know what the potential outcomes are and can thus assign some set of probabilities to those various outcomes. Uncertainty, roughly speaking, can be said to cover situations where not all potential outcomes can be specified and where probabilities cannot be assigned. This is often before the fact in which predictions about the future need to be made but this can be so after the fact, in which rather than predicting the future, an actor may be need to fill in the complete picture of the present but has no priors on which to do this, as when one lands at a cocktail party in which one knows no one and yet has to determine the occupations of the people in the room and how best to approach them with a networking pitch.

Almost every author in the behavioural economics realm, including Kahneman, seems to treat uncertainty of this type as something that can be modelled in a deterministic way and hence dealt with on the same terms as situations of low or no uncertainty. The neoclassical solution is to determine probabilities of a set of outcomes and assign those probabilities to outcomes to come up with a statistically 'expected' solution. In situations where probabilities change or when there remains something indefinite about them, the consensus view is that Bayesian inference is the appropriate model to use. This is based on Bayes' rule, which holds that: (1) the order in which information arrives does not affect judgement of a probability P; and (2) a belief in A (a hypothesis) can be measured by P(A) (the probability of A, a priori) and adjusted by evaluation of the new data, to arrive at an adjusted P(D|A), where D is new evidence and the whole term indicates the 'posterior' probability of A given D. Bayesian inference requires that these two probability assignments be independent (Camerer 1999: 10577). This process is posited as the optimal way (and most correct way) of assessing probability amidst uncertainty.

There is a great deal of discussion in the literature about how humans deviate from this supposedly optimal procedure. Camerer et al. argue that Bayesian inference is 'cognitively unnatural' because human beings are pattern seekers and the order in which they receive information naturally affects how they form hypotheses about the world and how they weigh evidence. In other words, whereas Bayesian inference requires independence of prior and posterior probability assessments, 'this independence is violated when beliefs about what is likely influence encoding of evidence, which is called "top-down" processing in perception and is manifested by "confirmation bias" in psychology (i.e. people see new evidence as more consistent with their beliefs than it really is)' (Camerer 1999: 10577).

So people are not built to assess uncertainties and probabilities in Bayesian terms. What do they do instead? One idea is that people use 'quasi-Bayesian' processes, i.e. people incorrectly specify the set of relevant hypotheses, or encode new evidence incorrectly, but otherwise follow Bayes' rule in assigning probabilities (Camerer and Loewenstein 2004: 11).

Kahneman argues that coherence, plausibility and probability are related but easily confused concepts and he finds plenty of evidence to show this. In particular he and Tversky found that even experts in statistical reasoning made errors in inference similar to those of non-experts which suggests that human beings have an in-built and commonly shared mechanism for making predictions about the unknown. Interesting is the finding that adding details to scenarios throws off even professional forecasters in formulating probabilities if that detail actually relates to plausibility (the logical notion that something could happen) but appears to be related to probability (the likelihood of it actually happening). Examples of such statistically illogical statements include asking them to rank the probability of an earthquake in California causing 1,000 deaths versus that of a flood doing the same somewhere else in North America (people assume the California outcome is more likely than the more general and more likely flood outcome simply because California is more associated with earthquakes), or asking them to rank the probability that 'Mark' has hair versus his having blond hair (obviously the former is more likely but people consistently predict the latter as being more likely especially given whatever details are provided about the hypothetical person). People routinely violate rules of set logic (where a subset of a larger set by definition contains a smaller portion of total outcomes and hence has lower overall total probability and yet people often assign larger probabilities to it rather than the larger set) and overestimate probabilities of statements that have greater salience or other characteristics leading to cognitive biases (Kahneman 2011: 159–160).

It certainly does appear that classical statistical reasoning does not meld well with human conceptual models for predicting likelihood. This is not to say that human beings are incapable of making good estimates of probabilities. Reframing things in terms more aligned with human reasoning processes can help. Kahneman (2011) has found that asking probability questions using words that evoke imagery yields more accurate answers than those that do not. That is, it is better to ask 'How many?' than 'What percentage?'. Additionally, people reason more accurately about frequencies than about probabilities, in which case it is generally better to express things in frequencies, not probabilities and to train people to translate probabilities into frequencies (De Meza et al. 2008: 62)

Also intuition and experience can be good guides to future expectations, as opposed to formal modelling but tend to be best where there is repeated practice i.e. short term things like driving under normal conditions. Long-term phenomena that take time to unfold, and unfamiliar scenarios, e.g. assessing future job performance or job candidate suitability, tend to lead towards natural biases and errors in prediction. This is why Kahneman recommends using procedures for assessing things like future performance of candidates using a list with a limited number of objective traits to assess, a total of six maximum, that are independent of each other and assessable by a few factual questions with simple rankings for each, e.g. 1 to 5, to limit bias (Kahneman 2011: 232).

A critical bias when uncertainty is involved is the **representativeness bias** which is where people overstate the probability of an occurrence by how representative they think its characteristics are of the general population, ignoring base rates of probability that are actually available and might well suggest different probabilities. Kahneman holds up Bayesian inference as the ideal here, suggesting that the proper procedure is to use the interaction between base rates and what the available evidence suggests to come up with a best probability estimate (a clumsy word 'diagnosticity' is used to describe this process) (2011: 146–155). Most of the literature follows Kahneman in this view.

Of course other biases come into this, such as salience. Kahneman reports on Nisbett and Borgida who found that showing individuals examples of people who seemed 'nice' and then asserting that experiments showed that these individuals are unlikely to aid others made a bigger change in predictions of how likely people are to help others than quoting evidence that has been validated generally and then showing individual examples. In other words particular to general is more powerful in increasing understanding than general to particular. And general to particular will more likely result in statistics being used to support preconceived stereotypes (Kahneman 2011: 170–174).

The **availability bias** is a closely related bias. This is the tendency in which memorable events are judged more likely precisely because they come to mind more readily. Of course memorability is due to many factors not related to probability such as vividness, publicity etc. (Korobkin and Ulen 2000: 1088). This also applies to personal characteristics, such as a whether a person with particular attributes is judged to be of a particular profession. Stereotyping might have a basis in this.

The bias has been well documented and certainly should be familiar to most. For example you may well get more fearful of plane crashes if there have been a lot of them in the news lately. However this bias is subject to change depending upon anomalies in recall because difficulty with retrieving instances of a phenomenon leads to understatement with the reverse being true of ease of retrieving instances. For example, asking a person to come up with six times they were assertive and then asking how assertive they were will cause them to think of themselves as more assertive since it is easier to mentally retrieve six instances than if they are asked for twelve instances (a number harder to retrieve), resulting in these same people to then think of themselves as less assertive (Kahneman 2011: 129–136).

The area of uncertainty is one where neoclassical principles, even 'bounded' ones, is arguably most deficient. Indeed some of the literature contains examples that seem to be written by 'Econs' talking down to 'Humans' and perhaps not fully understanding them at all. Very striking is Kahneman's discussion of his famous 'Linda', a stereotypical description of a person in which people are asked to rate the probability of whether she is a librarian or a feminist librarian, with set logic obviously suggesting the latter to be less likely than the former (since feminist librarians are a subset of all librarians) but with most people nominating the opposite. Kahneman sees this as an error and there certainly is a clear logic to this but this quote from his book is instructive: 'Remarkably, the sinners seemed to have no shame. When I asked my large undergraduate class in some indignation, "Do you realize you have violated an elementary logical rule?" someone in the back row shouted, "So what?" and a graduate student who made the same error explained herself by saying, "I thought you just asked for my opinion"' (2011: 158). This suggests talking past each other, one using natural language in a natural setting and the other using formal language in a contrived setting. It also suggests that there may be an issue with experimental design, i.e. Kahneman thinks he is asking one thing but it may be that people are actually interpreting things quite differently. There does not seem to be any controls for potentially different styles of thinking either. This is a more general problem with much of the literature which implicitly assumes relatively uniform styles of cognition across human beings and do not adjust for cultural and individual differences in expression, cognition, reasoning types and so forth.

Here is a quote that speaks, perhaps, to the different-ness and maybe the arrogance of experts. The naturalist Stephen Jay Gould described his own struggle with the 'Linda' problem, who in this particular case was given characteristics similar to an archetypal bank teller. Kahneman describes this: He knew the correct answer, of course, and yet, he quoted Gould, '"[A] little homunculus in my head continues to jump up and down, shouting at me – but she can't just be a bank teller; read the description." The little homunculus is of course Gould's System 1 speaking to him in insistent tones' (2011: 159). Could this homunculus be an introject from Gould's graduate training which is at odds with his more natural human inclinations, a conflict that does not necessarily mean the introject is right but that perhaps there are naturalistic versus formalistic ways of approaching uncertainty, each better adapted to its particular circumstances? Similarly with this quote from Camerer: 'Why is it so hard to explain something "obvious" like consumer indifference curves or Nash equilibrium to your undergraduate students?' (Camerer and Loewenstein 2004: 10) This in reference to the 'curse of knowledge'. But what is 'knowledge' but the result of training with not everyone being trained alike and not everyone thinking alike either? Getting a doctorate in something may make certain things seem 'obvious' but that doesn't make it necessarily so, and certainly not necessarily 'better'.

Kahneman and Tversky did an experiment analogous to 'Linda' using just sets of letters rather than natural language and found the same bias cropping up. Which confirms that the availability bias exists and can definitely distort perceptions and actions. But, especially in natural language settings, it is not always clear when and how it might be operating or even whether it is always an 'error' in these cases. Hertwig, Benz and Krauss (2008) for example asked participants which of the following two statements is more probable: [Statement X] 'The percentage of adolescent smokers in Germany decreases at least 15% from current levels by September 1, 2003.' [Statement X-and-Y] 'The tobacco tax in Germany is increased by 5 cents per cigarette and the percentage of adolescent smokers in Germany decreases at least 15% from current levels by 1 September 2003' (2008: 747). While initial questioning found the same 'bias' that Kahneman and Tversky found, follow-up probing showed a much greater and more accurate causal understanding of the statements suggesting that the initial answers were actually intuitively on point and perhaps more suited to real world nuances than a merely formal presentation might suggest (Hertwig et al. 2008).

This indicates that many behaviouralists may be too rigid in adhering to a one 'right' way to understand and posit uncertain scenarios, especially the strong preference for Bayesian inference and set logic. Just because Kahneman cannot understand the points his subjects are making does mean that their perspective is invalid. And many real world settings may not be collapsible into or commensurate with formal problem setting which by definition has to leave out ambiguity often found in reality.

The useful take-away is that there are times when people do indeed make systematic mistakes in predicting things and that people, even statistically trained ones, do not easily understand and/or apply formal probability schema. As an example behavioural considerations come into legal settings all the time, though not always thought of as such. Representativeness heuristics are especially important in determinations of fact by judges and juries. To use an example taken from Kahneman and Tversky, suppose that 85% of cabs are known to be green and 15% are blue and a cab is involved in an accident but the witness did not see the colour of the cab. When asked the probability of the colour of the cab, most people get that probability very wrong (1979: 1085, note 129). Legal practitioners may often thus be prohibited from introducing actual facts such as prior criminal background, probably because of the representativeness heuristic and this is a very valuable insight to come out of behavioural economics (Korobkin and Ulen 2000: 1087).

However risk and uncertainty in particular are far more complex than even the most sophisticated statistical models can capture and the rather primitive schemata used by neoclassical theorists is not a particularly good benchmark against which to measure human 'errors'. Another quote from Kahneman's book is instructive in this regard:

> The idea that large historical events are determined by luck is profoundly shocking, but demonstrably true. It is hard to think of the history of the twentieth century ... without bringing in the role of Hitler, Stalin, and Mao Zedong. But there was a moment in time, just before an egg was fertilized, when there was a fifty-fifty chance that the embryo that became Hitler could have been a female. Compounding the three events, there was a probability of one-eighth of twentieth century without any of the three great villains and

it is impossible to argue that history would have been roughly the same without in their absence. The fertilization of these three eggs had momentous consequences, and it makes a joke of the idea that the long-term developments are predictable (2011: 218).

This is obviously a very specific and some might argue absurd way of looking at things, a confident (perhaps overconfident) assertion that human society (in this case) is essentially subject primarily and almost solely to random fertilisation, gestation and birth processes driven by random Agents without wills in any important sense or wills that make any appreciable differences. It does show why Kahneman's approach to the uncertain world might be closer to those of most economists and far away from many of the people he studies and arguably typical reality. Which is not to say that he is necessarily completely wrong; but he is certainly far from completely right. His confidence is clear, however, as this quote about an interchange he had with a stockbroker indicates: 'He told me ... "I have done very well for the firm and no one can take that away from me." I smiled and said nothing. But I thought, "Well, I took it away from you this morning. If your success was due mostly to chance, how much credit are you entitled to take for it?"' (Kahneman 201: 216). Again, perhaps the overconfidence bias is at work in Kahneman just as much as this stockbroker?

In fact studied discussions of the true and varied nature of uncertainty are not entirely lacking in the literature. Kahneman himself has an interesting discussion of risk in his book, quoting Paul Slovic who says risk is human defined and variables meaningfully change according to the definition chosen, e.g. number of deaths per million people versus number of deaths per millions of dollars of products produced. But if this is so why then is Bayesian inference seen as the best way of approaching probability assignment under uncertainty with alternatives being seen as 'errors'? Cass Sunstein is more typical of much of the writing by economists and lawyers who do not seem to admit to anything but certainty in framing uncertainty, implicitly arguing that risk can always be rationally and objectively measured. Sunstein thus differs from Slovic, because the latter claims that ordinary people have valuable perspectives on risk missed by experts, while Sunstein thinks policy needs to 'nudge' people in the right direction towards experts (Kahneman 2011: 141–142). But what of the old story of the man whose son broke his leg – bad luck – who then did not get drafted – good luck – but then died in a house fire – bad luck – etc. whose main moral is to show that things are not as they seem and cause and effect is many layered and subject to shifting perspective as time and events unfold? Isn't there more on heaven and earth than is dreamed of in human philosophy?

An aside on Prospect Theory

Uncertainty is one area of behavioural economics where the neoclassical paradigm remains dominant with only incremental modification. Another is preference construction and determination, especially the construct of the utility function.

Granted that there are situations where an actor might know the relevant possible outcomes and their associated probabilities but how does that actor determine what is preferred by him or her? Behavioural economics follows neoclassical theory in positing that it comes down to selecting outcomes (consumption bundles, job decisions, etc.) that garner the most individual satisfaction and the utility function is the means for sorting this out. In other words, actors remain utility maximisers but ones who have certain limits that the pure economic actor does not. Jolls et al. (1998) says that the problem boils down to two types of biases: (1) judgements that systematically deviate from models of unbiased forecasts; and (2) actual decisions that often violate axioms of expected utility theory (1998: 1477). Issue (2), i.e. decisions that people make which do not conform to utility maximisation as practised in the neoclassical world, have already been discussed under the rubric of heuristics and Bayesian inference. Other types of deviations of this sort will be considered in discussions later with respect to bounds on maximisation and self-interest. For now some attention needs to be paid to (1), the issue of how actors make utility gain assessments that do not hit the sweet spot of optimality.

It is striking that the utility function is kept intact in most behavioural economics. Neoclassical economists consider this as a methodologically spare conception (a contention I will take issue with later). But of course an actual utility function has never been observed directly and it remains a conceptual invention. Taking it as a given and then adding some behavioural premises creates a need to modify it somewhat. What are the nature and shape of these modifications?

Choices are made in the dimensions of time and space. As already noted physical space is not really dealt with at all explicitly in the neoclassical model. Time, however, is considered, and offers two things for actors with utility functions to grapple with: time value and probability weighting. Time value refers to the fact that a resource received today has more value than that same resource received tomorrow. Nobel Prize-winning Paul Samuelson (1937) used the discounted utility model, which assumes that people have instantaneous utilities from their experiences each moment and maximise the discounted present value of these in totality. This was theoretically tractable but even Samuelson noted its psychological implausibility (Camerer and Loewenstein 2004).

Probability has two aspects. One, the determination of probabilities themselves, has already been discussed. The other is how to incorporate probability into the utility function. The neoclassical gold standard is the 'Expected Utility' (EU) model. Not only are actors supposed to discount utility according to when it is received, they are supposed to weight it in the present according to how probable it is in the future. We have already seen how deviations from the use of supposedly optimal Bayesian inference will throw off estimates of probability weights. It is also supposed to be the case that 'Humans' often add up probability weighted utilities in a way different from what neoclassical theory suggests. As Camerer suggests (1999: 10576), 'EU is the foundation of theories of asset pricing, purchase of insurance, corporate structure, and personal decisions like investments in education.' So it is a vitally important part of Homo Economicus. An alternative, hopefully with minimal modification of EU, is needed to augment neoclassical theory. That alternative is Prospect Theory.

Prospect Theory was developed by, once again, Kahneman and Tversky. It posits that people adapt to what they have experienced and then weight probabilities of those experiences nonlinearly. Both of these differ from standard theory which suggests that a proper weighted probability average is linear, with individual probability weights of all possible outcomes adding up to 100% probability and that utilities derived from experience are developed on the basis of net gains experienced. Adaptation, by contrast, implies that utilities are determined by gains and losses that are compared to some reference point, rather than by changes in overall net wealth or well-being, which by definition will be non-optimal in that if the former standard were used parties would be better off (Camerer 1999: 10576). The result is an overweighting of low probability events (perhaps in part due to salience, framing and anchoring) and choices that do not yield the most possible utility.

One author puts the contrast between EU and Prospect Theory like this:

> EU is like Newtonian mechanics, which is useful for objects traveling at low velocities but mispredicts at high speeds. Linear probability weighting in EU works reasonably well except when outcome probabilities are very low or high. But low-probability events are important in the economy, in the form of 'gambles' with positive skewness (lottery tickets, and also risky business ventures in biotech and pharmaceuticals), and catastrophic events which require large insurance industries. Prospect Theory ... explains experimental choices more accurately than EU because it gets the psychophysics of judgement and choice right. It consists of two main components: a probability weighting function, and a 'value function' which replaces the utility function of EU. The weighting function ... combines two elements: (1) The level of probability weight is a way of expressing risk tastes ... and (2) the curvature ... captures how sensitive people are to differences in probabilities (Camerer and Loewenstein 2004: 20).

The specific details of what a Prospect Theory based utility function looks like versus an EU-based utility function looks like is not too important for the purposes of this book. The major thrust is that even if people get probability estimates reasonably correct (and it is argued that they often don't) they also weight potential outcomes in nonlinear terms when a linear procedure would get them more actual utility. Some have claimed that there is some empirical validation for this. 'The similarity of indirect estimate and direct estimates [observed in various experiments] of caudate activity is not conclusive proof that the brain is weighing probabilities nonlinearly, but it is consistent with that hypothesis [of Prospect Theory]' (Camerer 2007: C34). However, Prospect Theory, like EU generally, is really a model of internal process, and relies on a very economistic notion of utility function. In any case Prospect Theory, while still one accepted model, is no longer the only alternative, though at the time of this writing it remains the most influential (Ramos et al. 2014; Brown et al. 2009).

Overall the literature exhibits a belief that messy reality is always (or almost always) formalisable in mathematical terms and thus 'solvable' in those terms. Indeed much of the literature reads as if it were written by those particular undergraduate students in technical fields who think in technical terms quite naturally, unlike many of their other peers, who then could not understand why everyone else didn't think like them. Differences in learning, cognitive, expressive, and emotional styles, to name but a few dimensions of humanity, are mostly not addressed in this literature. Essentially there is deemed to be the 'rightness' of formal approaches and the observed 'errors' (though possibly well-adapted evolutionarily) that come from non-formal approaches Humans use. Yet one could argue that this is a premise that needs to be deeply tested and debated instead of used as a theoretical premise. There are some obvious advantages to starting with a prior framework in the quest for understanding human behaviour but there are also times when a 'blue-skies' approach might save the time wasted going down dead-ends and this might be one of them. This is a point to be returned to a little later.

A final aside: 'stationary replication'

To close out this long discussion of deviations from the assumption of rationality, the repeatability of life events is another topic of debate in the literature. Experimental Economics, which uses artificial laboratory experiments to observe behaviour is considered by some to be a sort of 'gold standard' because the experimenter can theoretically control for extraneous influences and focus on the variables of direct concern. Agricultural economics is one discipline where this approach has a great deal of merit, as when two identical fields, one 'treated' with fertiliser, the other 'untreated', with all other conditions being equal, are compared to see whether the fertiliser (the control variable) is effective or not.

For behavioural economics however, the experimental method, while powerful, also has some important limits:

> Given that context is likely to matter, the question is whether to treat it as a nuisance variable or an interesting treatment variable … Economics experiments also typically use 'stationary replication' – in which the same task is repeated over and over … [but] … it is also obvious that many important aspects of economic life are like the first few periods of an experiment rather than the last. If we think of marriage, educational decisions and saving for retirement, or the purchase of large durables like houses, sailboats, and cars, which happen just a few times in a person's life, a focus exclusively on 'post-convergence' behavior is clearly not warranted (Camerer and Loewenstein 2004: 8–9).

'Stationary replication', in which the same experiment with the same subjects is repeated multiple times, when results converge or are stable, can be a good and certainly a useful measure of how people learn in highly repetitive situations. But these situations may not be too typical of economic life, e.g. buying a home (Loewenstein 1999: F27–F28). Repetition also tends to repress certain types of motives, such as fairness, or emotions. For example, how angry can one stay with repetitive scenarios? Ennui or boredom may be the result in those circumstances instead, though they may not be typical in real-world one-off situations (1999: F29). This is a recognised issue in the literature and is important to keep in mind when endeavouring to convert findings to policy recommendations.

Modification 2: Actors not being entirely 'maximising'

So much for deviations from rationality. It also turns out that human beings often do not maximise. Granted that neoclassical theory might hold that actors who don't maximise are by definition not rational. But in fact, a distinction can be made between the two for it is quite possible for even a clever and rational 'Econ' to fail to carry out optimal decisions if, as but one example, they do not have sufficient willpower to stick to their decisions.

Philosophically the whole notion of maximising is tied up with optimising. To maximise one must by definition achieve the best possible 'choice set', at least as far as neoclassical theory is concerned. Philosopher Jon Elster has pointed out that to be an optimiser people must know all available options, including those of the unknown future. The theoretical impossibility of the optimisation benchmark is thus obvious in an absolute sense (Etzioni 2010: 380).

Yet in at least a relative sense, optimisation is achievable in many cases and the dominant value system argues that attaining more material gain is better than less. Even if one does not want everything for one's self, one can use the resources for other desired objectives on behalf of others one cares about.

What would cause 'rational' people not to maximise? One reason is limited means to carry out decisions, such as bounded willpower. Another reason is patterning in the way actors set up the problems they then have to solve. This patterning could be considered as a case of bounded rationality as well but are considered here to be limits on maximisation instead since they are arguably rational in terms of well-ordered preferences with a particular logic that nonetheless does not result in that best of all possible worlds. Finally, and most non-economically, people may not in fact always want to maximise in the neoclassical sense. In other words their preferences are not maximalist.

Here is a list of the major 'anomalies' with regards to actors not always maximising.

Time-inconsistent preferences. Samuelson's model of utility posited actors having discounted preferences over time. Obviously 'goods' received later in time should be discounted more heavily than those received earlier in time, or so the neoclassical model says. To do otherwise would mean that people would prefer to have their goods later rather than earlier, and this clearly is not maximising utility.

Yet people have been observed to behave in ways opposite to this in many settings. What the 'shape' of their utility function is, what discount rates they use and whether they have a utility function is obviously a matter of conjecture but this discussion follows the literature in assuming that actors have discounted utility functions but discount in a manner inconsistent with standard theory.

For example, consumers often invest in less efficient heating modes because these are cheaper in the short run but more expensive in the long run. A 'heat stamp' program where consumers buy and accumulate nonfungible credits towards future supplies of oil has been proposed as one way of getting consumers to pre-commit and to overcome their time discount inconsistency (Pollitt and Shaorshadze 2011: 10). Energy usage is a field where time inconsistency is observed a great deal in which individuals generally highly discount future energy efficient savings, but appear to have low discount rates for current outlays. Inconsistent time preference is also seen as one cause of the inability to lose weight, to stop smoking, to save for retirement, that is, for any long-term decision that requires shifting of consumption from the present to the future (Pollitt and Shaorshadze 2011).

Also people dislike delays in consumption much more than they like speeding up consumption (Camerer and Loewenstein 2004: 28). And there is negative time discounting in which people may postpone pleasant activities and do unpleasant ones to get them over with. Note however that many experiments give noncomparable choices, e.g. getting an electric shock vs. kissing the movie star of your choice in one case. Thus all choices are seen as disembodied and embodiment shouldn't make a difference according to neoclassical theory. All of this is inconsistent with classical discounted utility (2004: 25).

One model proposed as an alternative to account for these behaviours is hyperbolic time discounting which implies that people will make relatively far-sighted decisions when planning in advance but will make relatively short-sighted decisions when some costs or benefits are immediate and they are then in the position of executing the decisions made in 'planner' mode. It is not entirely clear what is happening here but either people's discount rates shift as future experiences become present ones or, in static terms, present experiences effectively have higher discount rates than future ones, encouraging 'time-inconsistency in intertemporal choice' which is not present in the exponential discounting of the neoclassical model. '[S]omebody with time-inconsistent hyperbolic discounting will wish prospectively that in the future he will take far-sighted actions; but when the future arrives he will behave against his earlier wishes, pursuing immediate gratification rather than long-run well being' (Camerer and Loewenstein 2004: 23).

The economic development literature has actually grappled with this issue for decades. A standard story there is that people in underdeveloped countries are poor partially because they have preferences that are inconsistent with growth, having high discount rates or perhaps inconsistent discount rates so that is impossible for them to save and take the risks necessary to begin to accumulate capital. Risk attitudes also play a role here and are perhaps responsible for the 'irrational' discounting. Interestingly a literature review of behavioural economics in developing world settings finds that the evidence on the impatience of poor people is mixed. Certainly the available studies suggest that there is little difference in risk and time preferences between people in developed and developing countries and whatever these might tell us about other decisions they do not have enough power to explain why some countries lag behind (Cardenas and Carpenter 2008).

Endogenous preferences: *de gustibus est non disputandum.* Gary Becker and George Stigler wrote the classic neoclassical exposition of consumer preferences in an article using this Latin phrase in its title (which means 'the tastes are not in dispute'). They claimed that consumer preferences can be treated as exogenous for the purposes of predicting economic behaviour, and Becker in particular believed that all behaviour was economic in nature, or could be treated as such. However behavioural economics suggests that preferences cannot be taken as exogenous because institutions or other social arrangements can no longer be conceived of as being independent of them (Heap 2013: 991).

Most writers in the field have not really addressed this issue but if preferences are affected by institutions and yet also create those institutions in a simultaneous equilibrating process (or perhaps an evolutionary one) then the notion of maximising, at least at an individual actor level, becomes very problematic. At a minimum it opens the whole question of appropriate benchmarks against which to measure maximising behaviour. If the individual is no longer the basic unit of society, at least solely, then one cannot confidently say that the fact that this individual could have gotten more but did not in a particular instance is therefore not maximising. They could be maximising perhaps holistically, taking other relevant institutions and persons into account. Or perhaps they are efficiently adapting in a Darwinian sense.

Issues of self-control. Preferences are one thing, actions another. Perhaps people cannot stick to their optimal decisions even though they want to. One conception of this has already been noted: bounded willpower, which refers to situations where actors take actions that they know are contrary to their own long-term interests (Jolls et al. 1998: 1479). More generally people could be said to sometimes have difficulty controlling their self, much as a ship captain might have difficulty getting the ship to move in the desired way due to some defect in or characteristic of the vessel itself.

This can take many forms. Procrastination is, of course, a well-known issue in human life. Cognitive psychologists claim that present or immediate costs/ benefits are unduly salient or vivid in comparison with future costs/benefits. This leads to preference reversals over time and could be the source of high discount rates for short horizons and low discount rates for long horizons (De Meza et al. 2008: 22–23) Or, of course, it could just be a limitation in human agency.

A big issue around self-control is whether Agents are aware of the problem or unaware. Unawareness is assumed to naturally lead to less self-control and hence less maximisation. And if self-control is primarily a cognitive phenomenon, then greater awareness should be the answer to it. This is the basis for most public information campaigns. But awareness does not necessarily improve the situation. For one thing the 'curse of knowledge' may operate: you may know of your tendency to do something nonoptimal and therefore rather paradoxically decide to give in and do now what you don't want to do to get it over with (Tapia and Yermo 2007: 24–25).

And, of course, human agency is complex. Everyone can recount broken commitments and doing things that they did not want to do and did not even enjoy doing suggesting that the problem of self-control goes beyond mere issues of preference and knowledge. Bounded willpower may be too mild a term in some cases, echoing the Apostle Paul: 'For the good that I would I do not: but the evil which I would not, that I do' (King James Bible Authorised Version, Cambridge Edition, Romans, 7: 19).

Economists have been grappling with this issue for a long time now (moral philosophers for even longer) and it is interesting how much of this literature has not yet penetrated the behavioural economics paradigm. Amartya Sen's 'Rational fools' article of 1977 laid out a framework that distinguished between sympathy and commitment in which commitment (to a greater good and not just an egoistic self which might include others close to one's self but which nonetheless is still intensely personal) involves counterpreferential choice (to use Sen's words) and which involves significant self-control. Sen also refers to the balance between a person's social and private self, allowing in the social nature of humanity. This will be delved into when violations of the atomism assumption are considered.

The whole notion of self is sometimes interrogated. This notion posits that people do not necessarily have a 'unitary self' and that one self might make decisions in one time-frame but another self often takes over when the decisions are converted to action in another time-frame, overriding that earlier self. This has some subjective resonance but its use at the moment is largely ad hoc.

Intrinsic motivation. Because neoclassical economics is consequentalist the motivations of actors are inherently extrinsic not intrinsic. That is, actors do things to avoid bad outcomes and to attain as many good outcomes as they can. Yet human beings do have intrinsic motivations as well, things known to and important only to themselves and which may have no link, or even a contrary link, to extrinsic rewards. One can create tautological utility functions to erase boundaries between intrinsic and extrinsic but besides being methodologically questionable, the neoclassical model does predict that if offered a choice of satisfying intrinsic motivation while getting low extrinsic reward versus satisfying intrinsic motivation and getting higher extrinsic reward, every actor would choose the latter.

In fact, this is often not the case. When people care about money, their degree of concern is often remarkably unrelated to the amount of money involved. Small amounts of money can be more motivating in some cases, e.g. getting an undeserved parking ticket, than large amounts, e.g. a big change in share prices.

Context obviously matters as much as actual gains and losses. Experimental evidence also shows that pecuniary and nonpecuniary incentives can interact in still poorly understood ways, with, for example, big changes in behaviours in some games in experimental settings when prizes change in small ways if joined with increased knowledge given to all players of who won and lost (Loewenstein 1999: F32). The sources of these changes may have to do with human sociality, something to be examined in more detail later.

Intrinsic motivation is especially important with environmental issues. Frey (1999) refers to this as 'environmental moral' and argues that such motivation may be reduced by, e.g., trade-able permits, which may convey the message that it is OK to sin so long as one pays for it. He argues that both low taxes (which make consumers feel they have to stick to their 'environmental moral' or feel more motivated to do so to make up for the low level of tax) and high taxes (which make the activity expensive) are better than medium taxes which tend to crowd out intrinsic motivation without adding sufficient countering extrinsic motivation (see also Pollitt and Shaorshadze 2011: 19). This is obviously directly contrary to neoclassical price theory.

Even with monetary rewards, people have motives other than profit maximisation and these can conflict with one another, including the desire to behave in an appropriate fashion, conform to expectations of the experimenter, appear to be smart, or not stupid, etc. An interesting thing: people behave very differently in the presence of a mirror even when they believe no one is observing them. It does seem to be the case that maximisation may be an important but not always the most important objective even in purely economic situations (Loewenstein 1999: F31–F32).

Satiation. Related to this point, people do exhibit satiation, contrary to the rather clearly counter-intuitive notion of limitless wants (unless you have gotten your doctorate in economics and inherited such an appetite). For example, people's Subjective Well-being (SWB) does not increase after a certain point with income and wealth, which seems to be a clear violation of notions that more is always better (Heap 2013; Davern et al. 2007; Maldoon et al. 1998). The SWB literature is not behavioural per se but its findings have been invoked by behavioural economists and indicative of a potential anomaly.

Loss aversion. Loss aversion can be described with this example: someone who expects to earn 60 pounds in currency but actually receives 50 pounds is not as happy as someone expecting 40 pounds and receiving 50 (De Meza et al. 2008: 35). In neoclassical terms, losses and gains should be weighted equally so long as the net outcome is an improvement in satisfaction. Yet loss aversion is widely observed (De Meza et al. 2008).

There is some evidence that loss aversion increases with age, income and wealth and decreases with education (De Meza et al. 2008: 35). 'Myopic' loss aversion is the tendency to see risks in isolation, for example to imagine life as a series of small lotteries, with losses to be avoided, rather than a sum of lotteries with a total overall return (2008: 37).

Absolute versus relative changes. Neoclassical theory suggests that it is relative changes that make the most difference. A 10% gain in consumption should be worth more than a 5% gain and the absolute magnitudes involved should be irrelevant, unless one is at some minimum income or other discrete threshold such as a unit purchase price of a desired good in which case actors might be indifferent to 'in-between' monetary amounts. Yet it is clear that people's choices and preferences are affected by differences in absolute magnitudes, and are discounted differently across time as well. Thus actors may prefer a large absolute gain (or detest a large absolute loss) more than a smaller one even if the latter is larger in relative terms (Ert and Erev 2013).

Ill-defined or unstable preferences. Behavioural economists observe choices made but what are the preferences underlying these choices? Often the choices suggest 'ill-defined' preferences, at least by neoclassical standards. Some claim that although people often reveal inconsistent or arbitrary preferences, they do typically obey normative principles of economic theory when it is transparent how to do so (Camerer and Loewenstein 2004: 14). Seen this way, suboptimal choices may often be simply a product of bounded rationality.

Of course one might ask whether people really are being inconsistent. For example people may make one choice for one market and then a different choice later on and if we take a unitary self and a static world model as premises this can appear to be a contradiction. But why take a unitary perspective? Indeed markets change, which means choices change (including for new or improved products that didn't exist before) and it seems reasonable to think that preferences would change. Preferences can be seen as mutually created between producers and consumers (Heap 2013) This reasoning does, however, bump up against the assumption of 'exogenous' preferences and may present new theoretical problems. Perhaps for this reason it has not yet been pursued much.

Others have argued that markets themselves contain behavioural limits. They can create incentives for people to switch to more optimal behaviours but they cannot always force them to. Also not all things are subject to arbitrage processes, which is the way in which the market disciplines actors to move towards optima. For example an individual decision not to save enough may have individual consequences but the market will not do anything to correct it in most cases. This argument is really more about how markets cannot always fix human 'biases' and thus require some intervention, usually mild (Mullaintathan and Thaler 2000: 2).

Goal-less behaviour. 'William James, for example, wrote that "psychologic hedonists obey a curiously narrow teleological superstition, for they assume without foundation that behavior always aims at a *goal* of maximum pleasure and minimum pain; but behavior is often impulsive, not goal-oriented," while William McDougal stated in 1908 that "it would be a libel, not altogether devoid of truth, to say that classical political economy was a tissue of false conclusions drawn from false psychological assumptions"' (Camerer and Loewenstein 2004: 5, note 4). These short quotes provided by economist Shira Lewin (1996) indicate that human beings often do not have an objective in mind at all. And if there is not a goal there is no clear maximisation going on.

Reference-dependence. 'Standard preference theory... assumes that preferences are 'reference independent' – i.e., are not affected by the individual's transient asset position ... [and] ... invariant with respect to superficial variations in the way that options are described' (Camerer and Loewenstein 2004: 12). This is often violated, especially with framing effects. This could be considered a bounded rationality problem. It is included here because it also might be an instance where people have preferences that are not simplistically maximising.

'Status-quo bias'. People generally do not like changing strategies or behaviours and this yields what is called the status quo bias (De Meza et al. 2008: 44). This is a very well-studied issue in personal finance, and is one reason that Thaler and Sunstein argue that things like retirement plans should have an 'optimal' default savings option set to ensure people save rather than just stick to their current spending patterns. A variant on this is that an active decision be required by some deadline to avoid the status quo, with or without a default option, just so a person will not lazily stick to some suboptimal status quo. One author suggests that perhaps individuals be taught to frame their financial decisions as 'If I had to make the initial choice now, what should I do?' rather than 'How should I change from what I am now doing?' (2008: 48).

The source of the status quo bias may have multiple sources. The human tendency toward procrastination about unpleasant activities often leads to inertia. For example, sizeable percentages of participants in many retirement plans stick with their initial investment selection for many years and studies show that participants rarely rebalance their investment portfolios after joining plans. Some of this could be due to a desire to avoid the unpleasant connotations of such decisions, e.g. death and ageing (Tapia and Yermo 2007: 9).

The status quo bias however may also reveal a fundamental asymmetry in human desire, rather than a mistake to be corrected (i.e. a preference for less rather than more change) (McQuillen and Sugen 2012: 560). For this reason some treat the status quo bias as a property of true preference and not a deviation from it (561). This is something to be considered for all 'biases' which may in some cases be human tendencies, but not necessarily 'errors'.

'Endowment effects'. This refers to the hypothesis that people attach more value to things they already have than things they could have. Many experiments show that, for example, people will ask for more compensation for something they already own than for the same thing if they don't own it (Kahneman 2011).

This effect raises three questions. (1) Do people anticipate the effect? It seems not to be the case, i.e. people do not realise how much their selling prices will change before and after being endowed with something. (2) Is there a lessening of the endowment effect when goods are purchased for resale rather than for use (referred to as commercial non-attachment)? The evidence here is somewhat mixed. Some people do lose the effect if they trade in a good often as a commodity but not always. (3) What are the relevant 'reference points' for the effect, e.g. current endowment, past endowments or other measures, e.g. social comparison? People may use multiple comparison points, but how this process works is unclear. (Camerer and Loewenstein 2004: 17). Perhaps related is the 'disposition effect' in which people are less willing to sell a money losing investment than a money winning one even when tax law encourages the opposite. This could also be driven by loss aversion and also possibly mental accounting (considered later) in which people do not want to declare a loss to themselves (Mullaintathan and Thaler 2000).

'Gestalt' effects'. Another finding from the literature is that preferences towards sequences of outcomes do not follow in simple fashion from preferences for their component parts. People care about the 'gestalt' or overall pattern of a sequence in a way that violates the independence between the two demanded by neoclassical theory. (This may reveal a fallacy of composition in the neoclassical model in assuming that the whole is always equal to the sum of the parts and vice-versa.) A number of studies have shown that people generally favour sequences that improve over time. This can be possibly explained by savouring and dread which makes people reorder sequences to get undesired outcomes over with quickly and build up to more pleasant ones. Also people tend to adapt so ordering outcomes in improving sequence increases their utility because it works against them getting used to a particular state of affairs and does so by introducing slowly improving change rather than deteriorating change which is obviously highly unwanted. This also shows that people are sensitive to change generally (Camerer and Loewenstein 2004: 26). This could account for, and is certainly related to, time-inconsistency.

Complexity, ambiguity and lack of experience. Of course one may well ask what maximisation means in the face of the complexity and ambiguity of everyday reality. Some argue that this is what leads to most human divergences from so-called optimality (Korobkin and Ulen 2000: 1076). 'Work on learning in games has formally demonstrated Keynes' morbid observation on the "long run". The time required to converge to an equilibrium strategy can be extremely long ... The number of times we get to learn from our retirement decisions is low (and possibly zero). The opportunity costs of experimenting with different ways of choosing a career can be very high' (Mullaintathan and Thaler 2000: 3).

   This aspect of reality also may be the basis of most heuristics and the source of a debate about whether they are necessarily non-optimal (and thus could be consistent with maximising behaviour not opposed to it): 'A good heuristic provides fast, close to optimal, answers when time or cognitive capabilities are limited, but it also violates logical principles and leads to errors in some situations. A lively debate has emerged over whether heuristics should be called irrational if they were well-adapted to domains of everyday judgement ("ecologically rational")' (Camerer and Loewenstein 2004: 11).

   A more fundamental difficulty people have is knowing what their preferences are when they have not experienced the options before at all. This is another possible explanation for the status quo bias, as well as anchoring: it helps ground people and make sense of the choice they have to make. This may not be 'rational' or 'maximising' but it may be an intelligible response to a unfamiliar situation (Heap 2013). Sen (1977) refers to the innate nature of human desire for variety, which in this context may indicate that people may well engage in things simply to experience them, even if this may involve the risk of making them worse off. ('Why did I climb Everest? Because it's there.')

Preference reversals. This really is a label for any instance where people make one choice and then, for seemingly no or apparently irrelevant or trivial reasons, make the opposite decision. Many of these types of choices have already been discussed. They could be driven by: loss aversion (i.e. whether options are framed as losses versus gains); reference dependence (i.e. reference points change and thus affect the decision); status quo bias (i.e. preferences are sensitive to how the status quo is defined); salience of options (e.g. more vivid aspects of a set of options stand out more in a later round of decision making than they did in a prior round); anchoring (e.g. illustrated by this example of three choices: a week in Paris, expenses paid, a week in Rome, expenses paid, a week in Paris, breakfasts on your own. The inclusion of this last option shouldn't make a difference to choices exhibited because it is obviously inferior and yet its inclusion does make a difference) (Heap 2013).

There are many examples of this in the financial market. Quotes about long-term share market returns are meant to show that investing in shares is a good thing, especially if you plan to live a long time. But 'loss aversion' may cause people to have a good plan that they don't follow, as does anchoring and availability, which makes people cut share allocations after big losses for example, or during big price runs, the opposite of what economic logic dictates you should do (Thaler and Sunstein 2009: 122–123).

Mental accounting and choice bracketing. Many authors have claimed that people do 'choice bracketing' which refers to how people make decisions either narrowly, in a piece-mail fashion, or broadly, i.e. focusing on the 'gestalt' of inter-dependencies between decisions rather than the individual parts. People tend to choose, for example, more diversity of options when the choices are bracketed broadly than when they are presented narrowly. One experiment by Simonson (1990) showed that students chose more variety of snacks when they were given a broader choice for the week rather than the same selection just for the day. Also, people evaluating decisions in combination, when taking repeated risks, perceive the component choices to be less risky as a package than when they are evaluated one choice at a time. Thus a decision-maker who refuses a single gamble may nonetheless take that gamble when offered it in a bundle (Camerer and Loewenstein 2004: 18).

Related to this is the notion of 'mental accounting' in which although money is fungible, for most people not all money is mentally equal. So people will set up 'fun accounts' and 'rainy day accounts' in their head (and perhaps in their banks) and spend against those rather than against the overall balance. This can lead to 'nonoptimal' decisions but also can be a human way of 'self control' (Thaler and Sunstein 2009).

Satisficing. Satisficing is a term invented by Simon to indicate that people often aim for 'good enough' rather than 'maximum.' One supposed anomaly is a study of taxi drivers who need to decide how long to work each day. 'Pure' rationality would say work more on good days, less on bad ones. But many drivers set an earnings target for the day and quit when they reach that target, which means they often quit early on a good day, exactly the day which maximisation theory would say they should work the most (Mullaintathan and Thaler 2000: 4). (However this argument assumes perfect foresight and also neglects the value of leisure time.)

There are some satisficing heuristics that investors use, often referred to as 'naïve diversification strategies'. Benartzi and Thaler (2001) find evidence for existence for the '1/n' strategy in which participants split their contribution equally among 'n' funds offered by a pension plan (Tapia and Yermo 2007: 7).

People have been observed to use a number of techniques for making choices that are not consistent with the straight benefit-cost analysis of Homo Economicus. An example is 'lexicographic' decision making in which an actor identifies attributes that are important and then selects each one based on its highest assigned value, e.g. ordering main meals by price or taste. While globally rational, lexicographic choice does violate expected utility mainly because of the technical requirements for consistent ordering of choices and highest value choices overall. One example of lexicographic satisficing is 'Elimination by aspects' (EBA) in which the actor examines alternatives by their most important attribute, eliminating those not meeting a threshold value and choosing the option that remains. For example, eliminate all entrees costing more than $10 (Korobkin and Ulen 2000: 1079).

Kahneman asserts that there is a 'law of least effort' that says if there are several ways to achieve a goal people will gravitate towards the least 'costly' one (although he seems to say only System 2 makes 'effort' since System 1 is largely 'automatic', though this may in fact be a conceptual flaw). It is clear that human beings clearly do not always, or are not always capable of, maximising behaviour (Kahneman 2011).

Modification 3: Actors not being entirely 'selfish'

Human actors are not always selfish, in some cases having 'bounded self-interest'. As indicated above, it is not always clear what this really means in practice. Jolls et al. (1998) distinguish bounded self-interest as distinct from simple altruism because the latter is concerned with general issues of comparative fairness rather than a focus on specific individuals about whose welfare someone has concerns about.

The fact that human beings have a general 'justice' concern leads to both nicer than predicted behaviour (when people are trying to be fair) and harsher than predicted behaviour (when people are being spiteful because of perceived unfair treatment by others to others even if they themselves were not treated unfairly) (1998: 1479). Some of the effects that have been catalogued as a result of this phenomenon are provided below.

Voluntary public good provision. Traditional economics posits that individuals will not provide 'public goods', i.e. goods and services that have general benefits beyond private benefit because they are self-seeking, maximising Agents and will not willingly pay for anything but a direct gain to themselves. This results in the well-known 'free rider' of neoclassical economic theory in which a government or other collective has to step in to provide a public good through taxation or other forced resource collection because individuals will gladly receive the good if others will pay but will not pay anything (or at least not enough) by themselves and hence without outside compulsion no public good will be provided, or not provided in optimal quantity.

However, behavioural economics indicate that people can and do contribute to public ventures without compulsion in some instances and also modify selfish behaviour in the presence of certain cues that point towards reference points of general fairness or unfairness. The 'warm glow' effect is one example, in which people participate in providing a public good because it makes them feel better about themselves because they care about what others think of them (Pollitt and Shaorshadze 2011).

Behavioural economics also finds that people are 'conditional cooperators' and value fairness. Therefore it is not a given that they will never contribute to public good provision voluntarily. Traverse City, MI successfully built a windmill using a Provision Point Mechanism (PPM) in which voluntary contributions to a project are solicited with the proviso that if the benchmark amount is not collected, contributions will be refunded (Pollitt and Shaorshadze 2011: 16). One might also note current trends in 'crowdsourcing' and 'crowdfunding' of social projects by often anonymous or unrelated donors (Agrawal et al. 2013; Belleflamme et al. 2014; Brabham 2013; Estellés-Arolas and González-Ladrón-de-Guevara 2012).

Social norming. Behaviour can be modified when cues are provided about how people are behaving with respect to a general benchmark of overall performance by a peer group or by society. Door hangers that compared a given household's energy demand to that of their neighbours led to 10% more energy demand reduction than those given door hangers with general energy savings tips. Another study found that energy consumption increased when it was shown to them that their energy consumption was lower than average (the 'boomerang effect'). But this effect was eliminated when a smiley face was drawn next to their energy consumption. These were small studies but a much larger study found similar effects when letters were sent to users comparing their usage with neighbours, reductions between 1.11% to 2.78% from baseline usage. However it must be noted that this is still a small effect and it is not clear if it would be maintained over the long run. There is heterogeneity too: such a strategy works with political liberals but backfires with political conservatives (Pollitt and Shaorshadze 2011: 11–12).

Fairness reference effects. People have been shown to be very conscious of and sensitive to reference points of fairness with respect to general groups. In other words rather than just focus on their own selfish domain, people do have a concern with others directly unrelated to themselves.

Matthew Rabin has a formal model of fairness which posits three stylised facts about behaviour:

(A) People are willing to sacrifice their own material well-being to help those who are being kind. (B) People are willing to sacrifice their own material well-being to punish those who are being unkind. (C) Both (A) and (B) have a greater behavioural effect as the material cost of sacrificing becomes smaller (i.e. they are inversely related) (Jolls et al. 1998: 1494). The 'reference' transaction is the pivot around which this model operates and behaviour can be highly affected by framing and other cognitive affects focused on the reference point (1998: 1496).

In legal situations this effect may be the most pronounced. Jolls et al. (1998) note that 'Coasean' logic indicates that all that needs to be done is to set a property right to harm (or a right to be protected from harm) and the parties will then bargain to a settlement that is optimal for all involved, accounting for relevant transactions costs. But there are many examples of negotiations and conflicts in legal settings where 'obvious' optimal settlements are bypassed in the interests of perceived fairness or unfairness. Other cognitive effects can be at work too. For example someone who has received a court order in their favour may feel they have earned it and it then becomes subject to the endowment effect and thus much less readily bargained away, whatever economic logic might dictate. Fairness effects, in combination with this, may lead to much less bargaining than Coasean models would suggest should happen, with a resulting utility sub-optima by neoclassical lights. One way of accommodating this is to define transactions costs more broadly, to include costs such as displeasure of dealing with an adversary, though that could be veering into tautology (Jolls et al. 1998: 1498).

Unselfish game behaviour. Self-interest is often violated in the context of game theory experiments, especially in Prisoner's Dilemma games or competitive games in which players often 'leave more on the table' or act more cooperatively than standard theory would predict. Fairness concerns are often the source of these anomalies where people are trying to do some semblance of 'the right thing' (List 2006).

Once more there could be a complex of behavioural effects taking place. Kahneman, Knetsch and Thaler (1986a, b) put forward a 'dual entitlement' hypothesis in which previous transactions establish a reference level of consumer surplus and producer profit which then creates 'entitlements' on both sides so price changes that threaten this equilibrium are considered unfair. This could be an explanation for wage and price stickiness. Loss aversion among consumers and workers could be another explanation (see also Camerer and Loewenstein 2004: 28–32).

Modification 4: Actors not being entirely 'atomistic'

Finally we arrive at the assumption of atomism which holds that economic actors behave only with reference to themselves and their welfare (or the welfare of a few close 'others' the actor cares enough about to get satisfaction from their well-being). Already we have seen how this is not always the case, especially with fairness concerns.

But there is a more general issue here and it shows the divide between economics and other disciplines, especially sociology and social psychology. Note that Jolls et al. (1998) did not have a fourth category of 'bounded atomism'. Indeed, the assumption of actor atomism, though clearly present, is often not included in standard discussions of neoclassical assumptions or possible bounds to them.

Yet this assumption is often the subject of vitriolic attack outside mainstream economics. One author puts it most forcefully:

> Our common genetic-psychological endowment carried Buddhism in India as well as human sacrifice in Mexico; it was and is the same for the masses that attended the public executions of the Middle Ages for evening entertainment, and for the American citizens petitioning their legislatures against all political odds to outlaw the death penalty; it was present in Idi Amin and Mother Teresa, in Adolf Hitler and Martin Luther King and in Josef Stalin and Mahatma Gandhi. Only 150 years ago, well-to-do 'white' Americans found it entirely 'fair' economically to own slaves and entirely 'unfair' to force slave owners to let their property go; today their descendants find the idea of buying or selling human beings plainly abhorrent. I suggest that it is such differences that matter, and not whatever common substratum, biological or otherwise, may be underlying them. I also suggest that, to the extent that it exists at all, a common behavioural genotype as expressed in such widely different behavioural phenotypes cannot have much control over what happens and what counts in our historical world (Streeck 2010: 393).

This is an obviously strong statement, debatable in its particulars. But so are many of the statements made in neoclassical and behavioural economics (and the quote above can be contrasted with that of Kahenman, earlier quoted, about how people like Hitler arise and act in the world; the conceptions are almost diametrically opposed).

Here is a catalogue of some of the relevant behavioural observations of violations of atomism (though they are not usually characterised in this way by the literature).

Public commitment effects. People who signed a public commitment showed lower rates of increase in gas and electricity use than those who signed a private commitment (Pallak and Cummings (1976) in Pollitt and Shaorshadze 2011: 10). Along somewhat similar lines, cooperation increases when social sanctions are allowed and also when participants are simply allowed to discuss the game between rounds (Cardenas and Carpenter 2008).

Social influence effects. Of course there is a wide range of social 'contagion' that has been observed in both behavioural economics and in many realms outside of it. The 'Asch experiments' showed that people are more likely to make errors, or be less independent, when publicly exposed to other opinions and/or when they know their own opinions or assessments will be made public to the group. This particular finding holds across cultures. Social influence does affect outcomes ('obesity is contagious') and this can be used by 'choice architects' to 'nudge' people (Thaler and Sunstein 2009). There are clear analogies to this in the literature of financial crisis and of macroeconomics, such as Shiller's 'irrational exuberance', Minsky's financial instability hypothesis, and the 'financial contagion' of banking and economic depression, including the most recent episode of the GFC (Allen and Gale 2000; Minsky 1977, 1984, 1995, 1996; Shiller 2015). These will be discussed in Chapter 5.

Grass roots pressure, such as support groups for energy use (an example being an 'EcoTeams' case study) and peer comparison and pressure groups, have clear effects on behaviour in the energy consumption arena (Avineri 2012). There are many other examples in other arenas such as the use of small peer groups for professional self-certification, Weight Watchers and other groups for weight control, and active transport and exercise programs that rely on peer comparison and pressure. The effects are variable, of course, but they are real, and they violate atomism assumptions (Avineri 2012; Gneezy et al. 2011).

For yet more examples, conformism to 'peers' is very powerful and there is lots of evidence on this. For example teenagers are more likely to get pregnant when others are doing so and university roommates affect academic performance, etc. (Thaler and Sunstein 2009: 55). In an experiment in a tea room in an office people gave larger voluntary donations when an image of eyes watching were pasted above the donation box than when flowers were. Similarly people were more likely to vote for school funding propositions when the polling place was in schools than elsewhere. This process is known as priming and it is unconscious and almost impossible to avoid. It is, however, at the margins, some authors argue. That is, the effects are robust but not necessarily large (Kahneman 2011: 52–58).

In a corporate governance setting, many have studied the influence on Boards of Directors from informal norms and social networks. These can have as much or more influence than formal institutions (a finding taken up by the Higgs Review) (Huse 2005: S73–S74).

Authority and obedience. One set of authors has put corporate governance failure in terms of Stanley Milgrom's famous obedience experiments. These experiments involved putting subjects under the authority of one or two 'experts' (actually played by experimenter confederates) who commanded them to administer electric 'shocks' (which were not real but simulated) to people on the other side of a glass window (these people were also confederates). Although some of the shocks were supposed to be 'lethal' and the actors playing those receiving the shocks would scream in agony as the shocks supposedly increased, more than half of the actual subjects obeyed orders to administer those shocks to lethal levels despite having their own reservations and over their own verbal protests to the experts. Milgrom himself concluded that people had an in-bred tendency towards loyalty to authority, a useful evolutionary characteristic perhaps but problematic in some settings such as hierarchies. This result is indicative of how strong sociality is in human beings (Morck 2008).

Cross-cultural and cross-group effects. Though as of yet little studied in the behavioural economics field specifically, there have been some studies conducted in different cultures and these indicate the strong influence, and variability, of social norms in affecting behaviour. A literature review notes that college aged participants in the US show only moderate rates of cooperation which tend to decline in repeated games while cooperation rates are higher and more sustained among poor participants in Africa and Southeast Asia, suggesting the importance of cultural norms. Looking at only non-students, older people are more cooperative in the US, as well as in Russia and Southeast Asia. Interestingly, groups composed mostly of poor people actually conserve common property better than groups which are mixed between poor people and more affluent local property owners (Cardenas and Carpenter 2008).

The research also suggests that societies lacking formal institutions rely more on pro-social norms and preferences. Informal institutions may outperform formal institutions in such cases (Ostrom 1990). There are gender effects too. One study asked married Filipino couples to make family savings decisions. Men allocate less savings unless their wives can find out about their decisions, suggesting that either transfers intended to benefit children should be given directly to mothers or that mothers should know when money has been given (Cardenas and Carpenter 2008).

In summary, human sociality is a very important dimension of human behaviour and existence. While it is the prime focus in some fields, in economics it remains mostly a sideline at present.

Potential fixes to behavioural effects

This chapter will close with a review of some potential 'fixes' to behavioural effects that have been identified thus far. 'Fixes' is a loaded word, suggesting a buy-in to the neoclassical paradigm as a 'superior' one and typical behaviour as being in need of modification. But most of the authors in the field explicitly or implicitly make this very assumption. There are quite a few policy problems where such an assumption is warranted where human decisions create a social condition, such as undersaving, that could be ameliorated by different decisions encouraged through a 'nudge' or other behavioural intervention. In this setting the word 'fix' is appropriate, but it may not always be the right paradigm.

Because the 'Nudges' book is so influential, and so detailed, a brief synopsis of its solutions is in order as a starting point for a more general discussion. The authors begin with the concept of 'choice architecture' which is their term for structuring actor choices based on behavioural observations. The idea is one of design, like designing a car or a stovetop, an example the authors actually use (Thaler and Sunstein 2009, Figure 5.1: 87), to improve user experience. Design conflicts are inherent in many physical things. We respond to physical cues even if we know cognitively the opposite applies; for example, large handles on doors suggest 'pull' to open even if the sign says 'push', and people do pull even if they know you have to push. The key in physical design is to align the cues with the actual mechanics (2009: 83–84) Product designers and design engineers grapple with this issue regularly.

This analogy is carried over to a whole range of financial, economic and policy areas. The authors advise beginning with the findings of behavioural economics and adjusting choices accordingly, much as a product designer would adjust product attributes to maximise ease and effectiveness of use and minimise user problems and conflicts.

Let's take a very simple example. At the most basic level, human eyesight is prone to many well-known optical illusions driven by the way the brain receives and processes visual information. Even this human attribute, not behavioural per se, can have some potential policy implications. Thaler and Sunstein (2009: 38–39) note that the City of Chicago found that people were not slowing down on Lake Shore Drive despite signs ahead of a sharp turn that also indicated a low speed limit. So a series of lines were painted on the road which slowly got closer and closer together, giving the optical illusion of increasing speed to the driver, even when their actual speed was not changing, and causing them to reduce their speed more readily in response to the warning signs. Optics of this sort are particularly important in design on things like appliances, road safety and mechanical operation modules such as an airplane cockpit. And in this particular case it turns out to be relevant to choice architecture as well.

There is an underlying moral philosophy that Sunstein and Thaler join up with this and that is what they call libertarian paternalism (or what some refer to as 'soft paternalism'). This is very much in the tradition of 'consumer sovereignty' of neoclassical economics. This favours policy solutions that try to influence but not compel choices in a way that will make choosers better off, as judged by themselves and allowing them to opt out of specified arrangements if they want to. This is what 'nudges' are about: the idea is to guide people towards optimal choices but not force them into anything. One practical implication of nudges is to make abstract concepts concrete when presenting options to 'Humans,' e.g. not just numbers for retirement options available for different pension plans but pictures of lifestyles (e.g. houses, boats) associated with each level (Thaler and Sunstein 2009: 133). In fact, the term 'nudges' is an acronym for: iNcentives – Understand mapping – Defaults – Give feedback – Expect error – Structure complex choices (2009: 102). The overall summary of choice architecture and the design of incentives is presented thusly: 'Who uses? Who chooses? Who pays? Who profits? (2009: 99).

The book itself, and an associated website, contain many 'nudges'. Most of these aim to either neutralise or use known 'anomalies' to limit poor choices. Many of these are drawn from or are quite similar to private sector marketing tools. The difference is that social well-being is the ultimate aim rather than causing people to buy a product or service.

There are quite a few limitations to the 'nudge' approach and quite a few critiques of it. There is something novel and interesting about it and useful. But 'Nudge' has been critiqued, rightly so, as being very incremental and limited in its implications. We might design better airplane cockpits, for example, but perhaps we should be flying less, and a nudge won't help much with that. Sociality's power to transform individuals, for good and ill, is largely left to sociologists. This is very much an atomistic conception. Also in general nudges work best when relevant information can be abstracted, reported, measured and compared, but not all situations work like this. As one author puts it in the context of transport behaviour,

> Nudges work best on unintentional/automatic behaviours within a controlled context, however they are not designed to change the decision-making process of the reflective system. They do not make an objective improvement to the choice set or to the choices' attributes and utilities. Moreover, not like some of the traditional soft measures, they do not lead directly to a real change to the individual's knowledge, attitudes or values towards sustainable travel choices. It might thus be difficult to maintain and achieve long-term and sustainable behavioural change just by designing measures that are based on the nudge approach (Avineri 2012: 519).

This is the reason why the majority of nudges are in relatively abstract and static domains such as finance and less in more dynamic and contextual domains such as transport and environmental policy (Avineri 2012).

Underlying this model, besides basic atomism, is the notion of the perfectly competitive market and its processes that keep guiding people towards neoclassical solutions. Thaler and Sunstein (2009: 99) admit this as well saying that free markets are best when there are no conflicts between incentives. But sometimes there are such conflicts and 'Humans' (as opposed to 'Econs') may not always be paying attention or interpreting things correctly.

The moral basis of nudges is also not for everyone. It sits strongly on the libertarian end of the spectrum and while this approach has its merits, it has significant demerits as well. The other major behavioural economist, Colin Camerer, is even more libertarian than Thaler and Sunstein, preferring asymmetric paternalistic policy that 'creates large benefits for those people who are boundedly rational ... while imposing little or no harm on those who are fully rational ...' (Camerer et al. 2003: 1219) 'The goal of asymmetric paternalism is to help boundedly rational consumers make better decisions and align their demand more closely with the true benefits they deserve from consumption' (2003: 1221).

This may seem like an arcane discussion and many may think libertarianism as benign and well aligned with political democracy. But not all the implications are palatable. Camerer makes this statement as an example: 'The fact that suicide is currently illegal marks a classic form of heavy-handed paternalism (and is, in any case, difficult to enforce). An alternative policy suggested by asymmetric paternalism is to sanction suicide, but only after a mandatory cooling-off period' (2003: 1245). Which does not seem to be a consensus position and certainly not morally neutral. The morality and value set of policies is something that should receive more attention and explicit discussion, even if an overall agreement might not be arrived at.

Of course if human behaviour is suboptimal, or, worse, immoral, this may justify compelling human beings to do certain things at certain times, something not particularly consistent with the implicit value of consumer sovereignty. 'Soft paternalism treats anomalies as systematic mistakes or failures of self-control, and seeks mechanisms which protect the individual from her mistakes while still respecting her individual subjectivity' (McQuillen and Sugen 2012: 559). This is the basis of 'nudges' and draws from the philosophical concept of 'informed desire' in which a person's true desires are necessarily revealed in their actions only if they have unbounded rationality, cognitive abilities and willpower. If there is deviation then it is appropriate to do something about pushing them away from the actual desire and towards the more informed one. How strong this should be is a matter of opinion (2012: 560).

Yet consequentalism rules in the major writings. 'A crucial assumption in our approach is that the bounds on rationality – their range and implications, as well as which policies help – are empirical questions subject to systematic analysis, and thus cost-benefit judgements can be made' (Camerer et al. 2003: 1222). Cost-benefit analysis is explicitly focused on outcomes only, not on values or intrinsic ideas. These, if they are used at all, come afterwards.

There are many unresolved questions as to appropriate benchmarks for judging policy interventions. The big advantage of a nonetheless flawed consumer sovereignty model, is that one can take individual desires, whatever they may be, as the optimality standard. 'The immediate problem ... concerns what interventions are licensed. If choice is no longer a reliable guide to well-being, what is?' (Heap 2013: 994)

What are the alternative benchmarks? One could use the happiness literature as a guide. But then we enter a new problem of determining which is 'wrong', people's reports or their actions (2013: 995)? Another limitation of this literature is the implicit presumption that people want to be happy above all else. But this literature does offer some advice about policy prescriptions, e.g. taxing more highly those work-related activities for which adaptation is greatest and thus steering choices in the direction of non-work activities that have enduring effects on well-being. In other words, people should be steered away, at some point, from wealth-increasing activities towards others such as greater social life (2013: 995).

Right now these are noted as underlying issues worthy of further study yet not tackled much in the literature with some strongly debatable premises being used yet left unchallenged. Some of these issues will be considered more in the concluding chapter of this book. Leaving these aside for the moment, below is a list of some recommendations, in different domains, of policy interventions that are said to be behaviourally based and thus arguably effective. Not all of these are nudges and many are not drawn from that book. Some have more force than that. They do share a basically incremental orientation, working with existing systems and tweaking or modifying as needed.

Change default options: People are inertial, favouring the status quo and thus rarely changing 'default' settings (e.g. on a computer) so how the default is set is very important (Thaler and Sunstein 2009: 87). An example of default options are opt-ins and opt-outs to things like pension plans. A person can be given the exact same choice but framing it as one type of default versus another affects decisions. Thus it might be best to force people to choose an option if explicit choosing is deemed desirable (i.e. force people to think about things), such as leaving all boxes unticked on a form but requiring them to tick at least one. But this does depend on the complexity of the choice (in which case a yes/no choice might be better) and the technical expertise required (maybe computer programmers should set defaults on computers) (2009).

Examples of this are found in the fact that the lowest rates of organ donation are under explicit consent laws (opt-in) and the highest are under presumed consent (opt-out) (2009: 177–184) and the same can be seen in automatic enrolment in savings plans, retirement funds, with opt-out rather than opt-in defaults (2009: 110–112) (Thaler and Sunstein). Billing methods also have an effect. Increasing the amount that consumers have to 'top up' their accounts, such as for their energy plans, or making them 'exogenous', would likely reduce consumption since large top-ups are more salient than smaller top-ups (Pollitt and Shaorshadze 2011: 9). So if one wants to reduce energy consumption, this is a good mechanism for doing so. The same can be said of picking 'smart defaults' set by choice architects e.g. having green energy sources as the defaults (Avineri 2012). The choice of defaults requires careful attention and minor details can have major effects and even the set and number of options can have important outcomes so policy-makers need to think carefully about their design (Camerer et al. 2003: 1229).

Use present bias. Present bias can be used to advantage by offering small, frequent and immediate incentives for beneficial behaviours. Smoking by pregnant women, for example, was reduced by making frequent, mounting payments for documented abstinence. Other studies have incorporated social motivators such as competition and peer support (e.g. Weight Watchers) (Loewenstein et al. 2012: 1).

Limit and simplify options. Just maximise choices and information is the mantra of 'Econs'. But 'Humans' may really most need structured information downloads, not mass dumps, when choices are especially difficult or even just require a good amount of internal processing (Thaler and Sunstein 2009: 157). Choices that require more cognitive activity will result in longer response times and hence more likely to evoke an instinctive response, and thus one that may be suboptimal (Rubinstein 2007: 1245). Simplification of options and plans is therefore good because 'dealing with complexity and ambiguity is unpleasant' (De Meza et al. 2008: 29).

One might not necessarily just reduce options offered but simplify them, for example, combining participation and asset allocation bundles in pension plans, as well as reducing choices (Thaler and Sunstein 2009). Too many choices can lead to information overload resulting in use of default options for both high-knowledge and low-knowledge participants (Tapia and Yermo 2007: 6). Of course, one can provide sensible defaults but one should also consider providing simple choice sets too. There does seem to be evidence that plans offering more funds have significantly lower participation rates (De Meza et al. 2008: 40).

Strategically pick the form of incentives. It is argued that incentives are often more effective when they are penalties for non-performance rather than rewards for performance. This does not match neoclassical theory but is consistent with loss aversion in particular. Sometimes the incentives can be more effective when simply framed as a choice between a reward and a penalty; other times an actual penalty is more effective (Loewenstein et al. 2012: 2). That is, the form of the incentive matters even if formally the two are the same (One must question, nonetheless, whether incentives and punishments really are the same in actual experience and fact, although they may be the same in pure 'number') (Thaler and Sunstein 2009). Research also shows non-pecuniary interventions sometimes compare favourably to pecuniary ones. That's because rewards sometimes crowd out intrinsic motivation, especially if rewards are small (e.g. blood donations fell in one case once small rewards were offered) (Pollitt and Shaorshadze 2011: 7).

It is important to structure choices in a way that conforms to actual human cognitive processes and/or the positive aspects of human sociality. Financial incentives can detract from this. Incentives can cause people to consciously think about a narrow task and can shift people from broad to narrow focus, from 'automatic' to 'controlled' processes and away from social norms. It is not always the case that this is bad but it may be if the processes being turned away from are more effective or better for social well-being (Avineri 2012). Additionally sometimes incentives can be much smaller than the actual cost or benefit of an action and yet be effective. Some US cities have 'dollar-a-day' programs that pay teenagers with a baby a dollar each day they are not pregnant – which is immediate, salient feedback (Thaler and Sunstein 2009: 236).

One experiment involved non-faculty employees of a large US university. All were encouraged to attend financial information sessions ('benefit fairs') but some were randomly offered $20 as an extra incentive. Though set low, the pay had a large effect on attendance and five to eleven months after the fair there was a statistically significant increase in enrolment in targeted pension plans both for those receiving the incentive and those who were only informed that others in their department had been incentivised (De Meza et al. 2008: 13–14). In another case penalties for illegal parking might be seen by some as a probabilistic price that replaces a social norm and may be less effective (Avineri 2012).

One significant Law and Economics theory that might need revision in this regard is the Coase Theorem which ignores embodied effects such as the endowment effect and framing. In particular, assignment of property rights is not necessarily neutral because it creates a position where one party is a winner and one is a loser and we know this causes loss aversion and framing distortion which can lead to different outcomes depending upon the initial assignment (Korobkin and Ulen 2000: 1109–1110).

Encourage looking at things differently. Many biases might be ameliorated by requiring parties to view the facts of a dispute through the eyes of their opponents. This may be especially important in litigation. Indeed there are some trends in modern jurisprudence this way such as mandatory settlement conferences, court-ordered mediation, and nonbinding arbitration, which make little sense from a purely rational point of view but quite a bit from a behavioural view (Korobkin and Ulen 2000: 1094).

Use social forces. Sociality can be the basis of 'anomalies' but also a solution for them. 'Unrealistic optimism' which involves people's tendency to claim that they are less likely than their peers to suffer harm, can be reduced by exposing people to lists made by other individuals of relevant factors. Exposure of people to their own individual standing on risk factors, or of those of peers, or simply showing a concrete instance of an occurrence helps reduce optimism bias (De Meza et al. 2008: 60–61).

Other examples of the use of social forces are: 'application of justification pressure (the requirement to explain a decision afterwards and to convince another person which causes people to search for more evidence than they might otherwise do); counterfactual primes in which one provides examples that make concrete both an actual outcome (e.g. an accident) and the converse counterfactual outcome (e.g. not getting into an accident), which reduces confirmation bias (De Meza et al. 2008: 68); and group decision-making, which can be useful in de-biasing because groups can be a error-checking system, synergies can emerge from complementary expertise and the effective sample size of knowledge can be increased. Just simply averaging individual forecasts tends to reduce errors. However social influences can undermine these ameliorations as well as lead to them so care must be taken in specific interventions (2008: 60).

Interestingly the corporate governance area has seen some study of social influences, especially in CEO dominance of Boards. Not all of this need be irrational, as with information cascades, in which people rationally imitate a more informed player because they assume that person's strategy will yield better outcomes (and which may explain why popular restaurants are assumed to have better food, etc.). The Higgs Report in the UK however suggested that a firm CEO not chair board meetings, an attempt to change the framing of issues and reduce social influences (Morck 2008: 190). Weisbach (1988: 188) shows that there is more CEO turnover after poor firm performance in firms where there are more independent directors. Independent directors may thus serve a sort of 'dissenting peer' role. One suggested move is to mandate that future independent directors be nominated by current ones. Another is to have the CEO attend fewer Board meetings. Another is to let institutional investors or public shareholders nominate directors. Effectively this is changing the social pool from which directors are drawn (Maitlis 2004).

Explicit accountability routines are useful, for example having decision-makers imagining having to or really having to explain their decision to somebody else (De Meza et al. 2008: 55). A potential limit to this technique is that more accountability makes the decision appear to be more difficult and thus may cause reversion to heuristics (2008: 56). Accountability may also be most well adapted for some areas over others. It does seems to be especially useful in correcting conjunction error, i.e. adding up probabilities of different factors of a situation gone wrong (2008: 66–67).

Milgrom's experiments do offer some interesting, if as yet mostly untested, possibilities in corporate governance reform. For example, continuing administration of shocks fell off sharply when there were 'dissenting peers' in the room who began voicing concerns. This 'peer rebellion' was very effective in reducing obedience. Even greater effects leading to almost complete cessation of obedience were observed when two faux psychologists, similar in appearance and size, began arguing with each other about the effectiveness of the treatment (Morck 2008: 186). Thus even genuinely independent Board directors and chairs may benefit from an official opposition (2008: 197). These may lead to what Milgrom posits as an agentic shift in which people shift from having concern for outcomes to only having concern for loyalty to authority. This suggests a fundamental ethical/moral shift which is not currently a focus of behavioural economics, which is still implicitly amoral in the main (2008: 192).

A particular solution is to use conformity to your advantage. The US State of Minnesota gave four different pitches to four different groups about tax compliance. The one that worked best was '90% of Minnesotans pay their taxes' (Thaler and Sunstein 2009: 67). Norm manipulation is also useful e.g. inculcating useful norms, e.g. scepticism re: financial planning advice (De Meza et al. 2008: 69).

As a final interesting example, Ariely proposes a scheme where a borrower can choose to have emails sent to all their friends when their credit card debt exceeds a certain threshold (De Meza et al. 2008: 26).

Reframe things. Several studies about discretionary 401(k) plans in the US (tax-deferred retirement savings plans) find that the 'framing effects' of how investment and number of options are presented have an important effect on overall asset allocation (Tapia and Yermo 2007: 8). 'An implication of such effects is that re-framing a situation in subtle ways that would be irrelevant from the perspective of the standard economic model can have large effects on behaviour ... [e.g.] policy changes that require firms to re-frame their contracts, or provide seemingly irrelevant additional information. Such requirements might help irrational people make better decisions, while having absolutely no effect on fully rational people' (Camerer et al. 2003: 1230).

In an environmental setting one experiment compared emissions between best and second best transport mode emissions for a given trip. When framing differences in terms of losses, most participants perceived the compared travel options to be 'much different' by their emissions but did not perceive much of a difference when framed as gains (Avineri 2012: 517). State lotteries are an example of something that could be re-framed to allow for more responsible betting choices, for example expressing probabilities in terms of losses rather than gains, or using highly salient measures of probability such as graphical devices, metaphors (e.g. one ping pong ball in a pool versus a pool filled with them) and relative-odds comparisons (the odds of winning compared to being struck by lightning) (Camerer et al. 2003: 1231). Of course one might question the utility of having State lotteries at all, but that is a broader policy question.

Structure decision support. Simplifying routines used by people as choices get more complex is also recommended. Choice architects can help guide this. An example is Amazon's 'collaborative filtering' which shows consumers considering a purchase a 'you might like (what others like)' menu showing items that might match the consumer's desires based on their past purchases and the purchases of similar consumers. In a commercial setting this is meant to encourage more consumption which is not always what is socially optimal. So perhaps one should also be shown things that are unlike what we might want, i.e. that others not like us might choose, perhaps thrifty people (Thaler and Sunstein 2009: 98–99).

Utilise salience. Slogans that are highly salient are another effective behavioural tool though one has to balance the various biases that might get activated (e.g. 'Save 10% more' is memorable but not appealing) (De Meza et al. 2008: 69). Some behavioural prescriptions of a legal nature include: manipulating information given to jurors, especially information that would heighten biases such as self-serving and hindsight biases though this is not necessarily always completely possible given other legal values and requirements (Jolls et al. 1998: 1527–1528); alter evidentiary standards, i.e. the threshold at which a jury makes a finding; and increasing the 'probability' thresholds that juries arrive at for verdicts, at least modestly, to lower probability overestimates (and framing of standards is also key here) (1998: 1529–1531).

Salience is also important for billing. For example we know that sunk costs are easily forgotten and immediate costs are highly recalled. So the traditional incentive of raising electricity prices to lower consumption is a standard neoclassical idea. This should work fine but bills are generally received at the end of the month (or quarterly in some countries, like Australia) which lessens the incentive's salience. So better, perhaps, is to have the thermostat show immediate savings to consumers (Thaler and Sunstein 2009: 101).

Imagine alternatives. The planning fallacy denotes the tendency to underestimate task-completion times. A debiasing technique is the 'recall-relevance' manipulation in which people are asked to describe a plausible scenario, based on their past experience, that would result in their completing an assignment in a time-frame reflective of actual experience. This causes people to externally benchmark and adjust their internal expectations. In effect there are two types of forecasting: the inside view which emphasises the specifics of the case at hand and the outside view which brings in the statistics of a family of similar cases (De Meza et al. 2008: 60).

Re-train. There are many examples of where simple and explicit training can have a positive impact on choice. The sunk cost or escalation fallacy refers to people's likelihood to follow up on past actions as if they were not sunk (e.g. throwing good money after bad). Studies have shown that this can actually be trained away in financial domains (De Meza et al. 2008: 62) '[C]alibration training has proved effective in reducing overconfidence in professions like weather forecasting' (Etzioni 2010: 378, note 4).

'Learning rules' is a debiasing technique with two variants: (1) formal abstract training with the hope that people can transfer this knowledge to concrete domains: this has improved statistical reasoning for objectively measured problems and domains and also improved subjective judgements by making people hold off making assessments based on first impressions, making them see that more information was needed; and (2) learning a rule in a specific concrete domain with the hope that they can then generalise the knowledge to other domains (this does seem to occur over time) (De Meza et al. 2008: 62). Of course as with any education, the 'curse of knowledge' must be kept in mind.

Re-design disclosure. It is best to disclose things that are relevant and graspable (salient) and what people really care about. Along these lines Thaler and Sunstein provide the following formula for consumer information about financial instruments and service contracts: Record (show all prices, including every fee, in simple format), Evaluate (show people periodically how much of a service they used and all fees), Compare (show how their plan costs compare with other comparable ones), Alternative Prices (in which all service providers should provide comparable information) (Thaler and Sunstein 2009).

Provide cooling off periods. To handle impulse control and time inconsistency, cooling off periods can be useful. There are two types of cooling off periods: forcing people to delay action until after a specified period passes or enabling them to make a decision but giving them a period during which they can reverse their decision. These would not be behaviourally neutral obviously because of status-quo bias among other things, e.g. a decision made might not be easily reversed (Camerer et al 2003: 1238). Cooling off periods can also be used for bounded willpower. For example one could dispense drugs legally with a mandatory waiting period to protect the 'future self' from the 'current self' (2003: 1246).

Consider the opposite. A partial solution for anchoring is to ask people to 'consider the opposite' (De Meza et al. 2008: 64). The scholar Bent Flyvberg, whose work demonstrates consistent cost and time overruns in major public and private investment megaprojects, recommends correcting the planning fallacy through identifying an appropriate project reference category, obtain reference statistics for that category, and then adjust the base rate for a particular project time-frame and budget estimate using those statistics (Kahneman 2011: 251–252). One thing that can help, but not eliminate, optimism bias is what Gary Klein calls a 'premortem' in which, once a decision is made but not yet formally committed to, a team pretends to have implemented the plan and are to write a brief history of why it was a disaster (2011: 264).

Use decoys. 'Anchors' can be created by the introduction of a 'decoy'. This can be done deceptively (as with a sales pitch) or with a view towards lowering bias by distracting away from an anchor that might activate a bias (Heap 2013: 993). This involves placement of a seemingly extraneous but salient piece of information that might break up people's cognitive biases, if designed effectively.

Employ pre-commitment devices. Many times people need to be bound in some way to ensure they make good decisions. This is the essence of Thaler and Banartzi's (2004) 'Save More Tomorrow' plan which allows employees to pre-commit an amount to a 401(k) whenever they get a raise. (As mentioned earlier, 401(k) is a section in the US tax code used to designate a widely used tax-deferred retirement savings device for individuals.) Pension contributions are timed to coincide with pay increases so take-home 'losses' aren't incurred, savings do not start immediately and, once joined, savings increases are automatic. Also this plan starts with low increases rather than necessary ones, e.g. even if the need is to increase savings to 15% of income, nonetheless start with 5% and work up from there. Also suggested is to make financial planner appointments for people and not wait for people to make them. All this will increase self-control because it puts difficult choices off in the future ("start the diet tomorrow, not today"), and builds off of loss aversion, money illusion and inertia (Thaler and Sunstein 2009: 114–115). All of this has been shown to increase savings rates significantly (2009: 28). Other related ideas include automatic tax returns, effectively a default filing, and a 'Give More Tomorrow' for charity (Thaler and Sunstein 2009: 231–233).

Other commitment devices, such as Christmas Cubs, can help too. One thing that has been shown to help savings rates is elimination of the 'no decision' option, such as requiring employees to check a non-participation box for a retirement plan, something that resulted in a 25% higher savings rates than those with a non-enrolment default (Choi et al. 2004). The idea is that it now takes energy to *not* participate so people participate (De Meza et al. 2008).

Practice, practice, practice. Kahneman (2011: 11) talks about practice and how this improves judgement and quotes Simon on chess masters and how their intuition is not magical but simply 'recognition' based on 'cues' built up through experience into a knowledge base from which patterns are retrieved. So training is one corrective to biases and practice can be another.

Provide immediate feedback. Thaler and Sunstein (2009) found that continuous feedback on energy usage given by an 'ambient orb', dispensed to customers by a local utility, reduced peak demand energy demand by 40% (the orb glowed red when energy use was high). This shows the power of immediate and salient feedback (see also Pollitt and Shaorshadze 2011: 12). This is also part of the value of Los Angeles' easy grade health inspection reports posted on restaurant doors (consisting of a large 'A' as the best grade and 'F' as a failing grade) and the US Environmental Protection Agency's Toxic Release Inventory (TRI) which is a regular and simple report of individual emitters of toxic substances. For the TRI especially, it is suggested that there is strong peer pressure to improve performance (Thaler and Sunstein 2009: 192–194).

Understand differences in people. An interesting finding is that more numerate people are less impulsive, and more cooperative as the first mover in a sequential Prisoner's Dilemma (PD) game, more reciprocal as the second-mover in sequential PD, better at backward induction (that is, learning after the fact), and have lower discount rates in the short run. This may suggest that numeracy is important in better understanding formal rules of probability and perhaps in game outcomes (Cardenas and Carpenter 2008). Differences between genders, culture and age have already been noted. 'There is wide evidence of diversity and heterogeneity in people's responses to behavioural change measures in transport. Individuals' behaviours might be traded-off in the aggregated level, leading to so-called "asymmetric churns" making it difficult to influence, observe and monitor behaviour change' (Avineri 2012). So some tailoring of fixes in certain cases might be in order.

Use routines and algorithms in some instances. Paul Meehl found that algorithms do better than human judgement most times and this finding still holds (Kahneman 2011: 223–224). Kahneman argues that final decisions in many – perhaps most – cases should be left to formulas, especially in low validity environments. This argues against, for example, candidate interviews for top ranked graduate school applicants and more reliance on statistical measures ranked by simple formula. (It must be remembered that humans make the algorithms. So stating a preference for algorithms may be rather like saying that robots are better than the humans who programmed them. It also assumes that everything most important is measurable. These are issues that merit some further work.) Robyn Dawes goes a step further and says that simple formulas without prior statistical knowledge often work better than those with such knowledge. One example: marital stability = lovemaking frequency – quarrel frequency (in Kahneman 2011: 226). In other words standardised procedure is often a good thing to use to minimise human error.

Overall there are quite a few concrete recommendations for policy recommendations that arise from the behavioural economics literature. Some of these have been implemented or experimented with in some actual settings. The design of Personal Account Pensions in the UK has, for example, been much influenced by David Laibson's work on defaults (De Meza et al. 2008: 8). The

UK Cabinet Office (Dolan et al. 2012) posits the MINDSCAPE framework (Messenger, Incentives, Norms, Defaults, Salience, Priming, Affect, Commitments, Ego). While the UK Department for Transport is finalising a Behavioural Insights toolkit to support better choices by travellers (Avineri 2012).

What of the potential for corporate governance? To this issue the next three chapters turn.

4 Corporate governance failures and malfunctions

Their etiologies

Boundary issues

Every decade since the late 19th century seems to witness its share of major corporate governance scandals and failures. Some of these morph and blend into (or are perhaps caused by) large-scale economic disruptions such as the Great Depression of the 1930s or the Global Financial Crisis (GFC) of the 2000s, to say nothing of the now forgotten worldwide 'panics' of 1871, 1893 and 1907 (Kindleberger and Aliberger 2011).

This recurrence would suggest that there is a systemic pattern to the modern economy and corporate form that makes crisis and collapse inevitable, or at least to be expected. Yet prescriptions for corporate governance since the 1930s, when the issue began to be addressed in a more formal way, often read as if cycles of collapse and disorder could be reduced to the occasional accident, like airplane crashes in modern air travel, if only certain protocols were followed and enforced. Indeed, corporate failures lead to forensic investigations that read like aviation safety recommendations in their precision and degree of certainty. However, while air crashes have indeed become statistically rare as a result of learning from past mistakes, corporate crashes seem as common as ever. And their causes seem recurrent.

This chapter will briefly tease out some broad recurrent themes of corporate governance scandal and failure in the modern era and consider the policy and academic thinking and legislative response that has paralleled it. The focus will be on corporate governance occurrences that suggest an agency problem. Some things defined as bad governance by policy-makers and society may nonetheless be consistent with utility maximisation and alignment of Principal and Agent economic interests, even if nefarious in means, such as bribery of government officials to secure lucrative corporate contracts. These actions may be illegal, or immoral, but may nevertheless maximise shareholder value and from that standpoint an Agent may be doing the job that they were hired for in a very narrow sense. If a corporate manager wants to bribe an official or donate to a political campaign and this will potentially help the corporation's owners, then the neoclassical perspective would call for the calculation of the benefits and costs of doing so, including the potential costs and probabilities of getting caught weighed against the probabilities of a successful payoff. If that calculation increases NPV (Net Present Value) then it would be irrational not to go forward.

Of course this is not a neoclassical world and one may thank one's lucky stars for that. The reason for this narrow and even socially absurd analytical focus here is not to justify illegal or immoral activity, but because such a focus sticks closest to the neoclassical Governance Theory with behavioural amendments that is the concern of this book. Additionally it hopefully avoids the thickets of some ideological and philosophical debates about the proper scope of corporate governance such as Corporate Social Responsibility (CSR). These boundary issues will be examined more fully in the final chapter.

Recurrent themes in corporate governance failure

A complete review of the corporate governance misfires that have resulted in destruction of shareholder value is obviously not to be attempted here. However the stylised facts do suggest that the modern corporate form is highly subject to them. Table 4.1 provides some of the highlights (or low lights if one prefers) over the past 120 years or so in the Anglo-American world (mostly the US and the UK with some Australian and Canadian examples thrown in). A less extensive selection of corporate scandals from the rest of the world is provided in Table 4.2, covering the last three decades.

This tabular review focuses on failures and scandals because they are most dramatic and lay bare corporate fundamental governance issues. They do have the disadvantage of being 'dead' not living phenomena and representative of extremes that may not conform with everyday norms. There is no doubt a lot of governance malfunction that takes place regularly but which is not bad enough, or which is covered over by favourable economic conditions, to cause obvious problems, yet which still results in inefficiency. Conversely, there may be a lot of good governance that does not call attention to itself in the midst of the occasional and dramatic malfunction. Either way the malfunctions are bad and frequent enough to indicate to most observers that there is a problem that remains to be solved.

These tables could obviously have been much, much longer in their listing of individual examples of corporate failure due to poor governance. And to understand the magnitude of corporate governance malfeasance, some normalisation is needed, such as a scaling of shareholder value lost relative to total shareholder worth for a given firm or a measure of impacts of firm failures relative to Gross Domestic Product. Interestingly not much of this type of analysis is available. A normalisation like this might show the governance problem to be less significant than the tables make them appear, or it might buttress their anecdotal magnitude. What should be obvious, however, is that corporate failure and scandal of significant scale is a regular occurrence and often tied to major economic upheaval.

Remember that this list does not focus on the numerous examples of corporate wrongdoing and illegal activity that could be seen as consistent with an alignment of Principals and Agents but which is just overly aggressive, for example the

Table 4.1 Major corporate governance scandals/failures in the Anglo–American business world since 1900 (selected)

Decade(s)	Example	Country	Cause/Type	Sector	Economic setting	References
1900s	Rise and instability of the industrial 'trust' companies (1907)	USA, worldwide	Pyramid financial and corporate structures, cross-holdings and self-dealing	Industrial, manufacturing, financial	Panic of 1907	Frydman et al. 2012
1920s	Hatry Group collapse (1929)	UK	Issuance of fraudulent securities, used as collateral	Finance	'Boom' of the 1920s (collapse just prior to the 1929 stock market crash)	Roberts 2008
	Investment Trusts	US	'Watered' shares and pyramided structures to issue under-capitalised shares	Finance, Industrial	'Boom' of the 1920s	Galbraith 2009
1930s	Ivar Kruegar (the Match King) business collapse and Kruegar suicide (1932)	US Europe (Swedish company with major loans and contracts with European governments)	Financial manipulation, accounting fraud and irregularity, uncontrolled risk taking and leveraging	Matches	Great Depression	MacNeal 1939
	Interstate Hosiery Mills scandal (1937)	USA	Fraudulent share manipulation	Apparel	Great Depression	MacNeal 1939
	McKesson & Robbins, Inc. scandal (1938)	USA	Major mis-appropriation of funds by executives; assumption of false identities	Pharmaceutical	Great Depression	MacNeal 1939
1950s	The 'Quiz Show' scandal – CBS broadcasting (1955–1957)	USA	Major US network (CBS) rigged TV quiz show	Television broadcasting	Postwar recovery and prosperity	Anderson 1978

Decade	Event	Country	Description	Sector	Economic context	Reference
1960s	Great Salad Oil Scandal (bankruptcy of Allied Crude Vegetable Oil Refining Co.) (1963) Securities market repercussions	USA	False collateral based on nonexistent inventories of vegetable oil to secure loans from 51 major corporations; lack of due diligence by lenders	Food (vegetable oil) Other corporate sectors (lenders)	1960s prosperity	Taylor 2013
1970s	Penn Central Railroad bankruptcy (1970)	USA	Accounting irregularities, excessive risk taking, poor internal controls	Transport, conglomerate	'Stagflation' (corporate commercial paper crisis triggered by crisis and preceded by commercial paper boom)	Salisbury 1982
	National Student Marketing Corporation scandal (1970)	USA	Securities fraud	Education marketing	'Go go' share market boom followed by stagflation	Labaton 1986
1980s	Savings and Loan Crisis (mid- to late 1980s)	USA	Major collapse of financial institutions, partly due to interest rate environment, partly due to fraud at particular institutions (e.g. Charles Keating)	Finance	High interest rates following major inflation and tight money policy by US central bank. Economic recovery	Calavita et al. 1997

Table 4.1 continued

Decade(s)	Example	Country	Cause/Type	Sector	Economic setting	References
1990s	Polly Peck failure (1990)	UK	Embezzlement, accounting fraud	Textiles		Mitchell et. al. 1994
	Bank of Credit and Commerce International (BCCI) failure (1991)	UK	Money laundering, financial fraud	Finance		Herring 1993
	Maxwell Group scandal and collapse (1991)	UK	Misappropriation and theft from corporate pension funds	Press and newspapers		Stiles and Taylor 1993
	Barings Bank collapse (1995)	UK	'Rogue' trader taking unsecured positions; poor internal controls	Finance		Roberts 2008
	Sunbeam Corporation (1998)	USA	Major accounting misstatements	Appliances	Sharemarket boom	Ketz 2003
	Waste Management Inc. (1998)	USA	Major accounting misstatements	Waste management	Sharemarket boom	Ketz 2003
	Cedant Corporation (1998)	USA	Accounting and financial fraud	Diversified		Vogel 2001, Ketz 2003
	Long-Term Capital Management (LTCM) failure, bankruptcy and major bailout	USA	Excesssive risk-taking, poor risk controls	Finance	Asian Financial Crisis of 1998	Edwards 1999, Mackenzie 2003

Decade	Event	Country	Description	Industry		Reference
2000s	Equitable Life Assurance Society Failure (2000)	UK	Unlawful misappropriation of funds held in trust by annuity holders to cover current annuity payments	Finance		O'Brien 2006
	Enron Bankrupcty (2001)	USA	Major accounting and financial fraud, self-dealing	Energy		Lease 2006
	Worldcom bankruptcy (2002)	USA	Major accounting and financial fraud, self-dealing	Telecommunications		Lease 2006
	HIH bankruptcy (2001)	Australia	Fraud, poor risk management	Insurance		Watts 2002
	Tyco International Scandal (2002)	USA	Theft and misappropriation of corporate resources by top management	Technology – diversified		Lease 2006
	Hollinger International (Conrad Black) scandal (2003)	Canada	Major financial fraud and accounting irregularities	Newspapers		CBC News 2010
	Lehman Brothers Bankruptcy 15 September 2008	USA	Excessive risk-taking and accounting irregularities: received unqualified audit opinion months before failure	Finance	Global Financial Crisis	Lipman 2012
	American International Group TARP 9/16/2008	USA	Excessive risk-taking and accounting irregularities: received unqualified audit opinion months before failure	Finance	Global Financial Crisis	Lipman 2012
	Citigroup TARP 26 October 2008	USA	Excessive risk-taking and accounting irregularities: received unqualified audit opinion months before failure	Finance	Global Financial Crisis	Lipman 2012

Table 4.1 continued

Decade(s)	Example	Country	Cause/Type	Sector	Economic setting	References
	Fannie Mae Government takeover 6 September 2008	USA	Excessive risk-taking and accounting irregularities: received unqualified audit opinion months before failure	Finance	Global Financial Crisis	Lipman 2012
	Freddie Mac Government takeover 2 September 2008	USA	Excessive risk-taking and accounting irregularities: received unqualified audit opinion months before failure	Finance	Global Financial Crisis	Lipman 2012
	Washington Mutual Bankruptcy 26 September 2008	USA	Excessive risk-taking and accounting irregularities: received unqualified audit opinion months before failure	Finance	Global Financial Crisis	Lipman 2012
	New Century Financial Corp. Bankruptcy 2 April 2007	USA	Excessive risk-taking and accounting irregularities: received unqualified audit opinion months before failure	Finance	Global Financial Crisis	Lipman 2012
	The Bear Stearns Companies Inc. Purchased 17 March 2008	USA	Excessive risk-taking and accounting irregularities: received unqualified audit opinion months before failure	Finance	Global Financial Crisis	Lipman 2012
	Countrywide Financial Corp. Purchased 11 January 2008	USA	Excessive risk-taking and accounting irregularities: received unqualified audit opinion months before failure	Finance	Global Financial Crisis	Lipman 2012

Table 4.2 Selected corporate governance scandals/failures in non-English speaking countries since 2000

Example	Country	Cause/Type	Sector	Economic setting	References
Parmalat failure (2003)	Italy	Accounting fraud, theft of company funds	Diversified	Strong economic growth	Melis 2005
Vivendi Universal (2002–2003)	France	Accounting irregularity and embezzlement	Media	Strong economic growth	Clark 2004
Sanlu Group (2008)	China	Product adulteration (melamine added to formula)	Infant formula	Global Financial Crisis	Rajagopalan and Zhang 2009
Satyam Computer Services (2008)	India	Major accounting fraud and financial statement analysis		Global Financial Crisis	Rajagopalan and Zhang 2009
Olympus (2011)	Japan	Major financial fraud and concealment of losses	Optimal equipment	Global Financial Crisis recovery	Binham 2011

foreign bribery scandals and the illegal corporate campaign donations to the Richard Nixon presidential re-election campaign that occurred in the US in the 1970s and led to significant new domestic laws in both those areas. The cases above are examples of theft of shareholder resources by managers and related accounting and financial fraud, misappropriation, poor internal controls and excessive and uncontrolled and unmonitored risk taking. Bankruptcy wiping out shareholders and bondholders were often the result.

A few major themes stand out from the history and the literature. (Suspected causes are addressed more systematically in the following section.)

Risk mismanagement. Business is inherently risky and failure is always a clear and present possibility. Handling the tradeoff between risk and potential reward in ways consistent with strategic reality and shareholder risk appetite is a key task of internal governance. Yet many times companies fail extremely badly at striking this balance. Enron was a graphic example of management that took overly aggressive risk positions and committed major fraud in doing so, in the form of extreme accounting legerdemain and the creation of sham financial entities designed to both falsely boost reported earnings and enrich executives, especially the company Chief Financial Officer (CFO). The recent Global Financial Crisis is rife with banks that lowered credit standards extremely and misled borrowers about the nature of the mortgage loans being extended to them along with investment firms that packaged mortgages in ways that were meant to hide credit risk, with both types of entities manipulating financial statements in an extreme manner. Striking is that fact that many of these companies had risk management officers or departments that were either ignored or failed to do adequate analysis. Not all failures are of this type, but risk management mishandling and malfeasance are regular occurrences.

The role of finance. Closely linked to corporate risk profile is the type of financing and level of debt that managers choose to employ. Failures and scandals linked to corporate finance tend to be of two major types: overly leveraged firms and share price manipulation. Often these two are linked as managers may take on borrowed capital to indirectly or fraudulently boost the accounts and thus raise share prices, often using these shares as a currency for mergers and acquisitions and collateral and then plugging financial statement holes with these ill-gotten gains. Many companies during 'boom' periods right before 'busts' fell into malfeasance of this sort, e.g. the stock manipulation scandals that led to and were unwound by the Stock Market Crash of 1929 in the US and around the world, and the fall of the various corporate 'darlings' of the 'tech bubble' in sharemarkets during the share run-up in the 1990s that ended in the market recession of 2000s (Enron, Worldcom, Global Crossing and many others being in this camp to varying degrees). The choice of company capital structure is obviously a management prerogative but the proper idea is to choose a debt/equity composition that is most efficient from a shareholder value perspective (at least according to neoclassical theory), not willful manipulation of financial statements and positions to boost executive compensation.

Macroeconomic cycles. Obviously the economic cycle is critical to corporate success and corporate governance. Of course a well-run company may fail because of bad economic timing, or a badly run company may succeed because of good economic timing. The issue is how governance is affected by and affects the macroeconomic cycle. Economic booms, especially sharemarket booms, are highly correlated with governance misfires that result in firm crisis. Theories about cause and effect will be considered a little later. But general economic conditions do seem to affect, at least indirectly, management decisions and shareholder attitudes about risk, business strategy and corporate policy in ways that sometimes lead to problems.

Sectoral influences. Firms do not operate in isolation and sometimes the line of business they are in affects the type of governance structure they choose and the problems they fall into. The financial services sector has its own unique set of issues but others can fall into this pattern, as the industrial and consumer services conglomeration wave of the 1960s, the high tech 'bubble' at the turn of the millennium and the railroad booms and busts of the late 19th and early 20th centuries all indicate. Of course sectoral changes are closely interwoven with macroeconomics. In any case waves of governance and organisational 'fads' are clearly present.

Charismatic leaders. A common theme in some failures is the excess and inordinate sway of a particular individual at the company helm. Family run and closely held companies such as Parmalat are obvious candidates for this problem but it is amazing how often large public companies fall into this trap. Dennis Kowzlowski at Tyco, Jeffrey Skilling at Enron, and Conrad Black at Hollinger are but a few of myriad examples of CEOs who took their companies hostage despite the presence of supposedly sophisticated shareholders, independent Board members and reputable gatekeepers. This is one particularly human foible in corporate governance and arguably an example that behavioural approaches might explain much better than purely rationally based models.

Some standard diagnoses and recommendations

These are general points, but what about specific proposals for reducing the incidence of corporate failures? When diagnosing the causes of recurrent governance problems, the literature fairly closely follows standard theory in identifying potential cause and effect. The starting premise it that shareholders are the primary Principals of a firm and that their interests and imperatives must be carried out by Agents. Most standard diagnoses flow from this on to the following major dimensions.

- Composition and independence of the Board of Directors
- Board of Directors structure
- Role of the CEO
- Structure and composition of shareholdings
- Executive compensation
- Independence and nature of 'gatekeepers'
- Legal and regulatory environment
- Social and other norms and institutions
- Strength of external market forces ('the market for corporate control').

To consider each in turn, a very large amount of attention has been paid to the role of the Board of Directors and the CEO. After a rash of corporate scandals in the UK, the Cadbury Report (that is, the Report of the UK Committee on the Financial Aspects of Corporate Governance, chaired by Sir Adrian Cadbury, former Chairman of Cadbury Schweppes and a director of the Bank of England) was published in 1992 and made extensive recommendations on corporate Board structure. In particular it was suggested that at least three independent non-executive directors (NEDs) should serve on a company Board and that NEDs should be the sole or dominant representatives on two committees that all Boards should have, audit and remuneration, both responsible to the board directly. Establishment of a nomination committee was also suggested to ensure the transparency and integrity of the appointment of new directors. As for what 'independent' means, the Cadbury Report states that: '[A]apart from their directors' fees and shareholdings, they [directors] should be independent of management and free from any business or other relationship which could materially interfere with the exercise of their independent judgment.' Additionally,

CEO and Chair roles should always be separate. These recommendations were incorporated into later UK legislation addressing a wide range of corporate governance aspects (Mallin et al. 2005).

These themes arose again in the wake of the Global Financial Crisis a decade later. For example, an OECD analysis of governance lessons from that crisis noted that genuine independence of directors, membership on Board committees, and Board access to information were, especially with regards to risk management, recurrent issues prior to the crisis (Kirkpatrick 2009). The criteria used for defining independence were difficult to define and implement effectively and it was suggested that purely 'negative' criteria might need to be supplemented with positive and definite examples of what independence looks like.

Closely linked to independence is director competence and experience, something the Cadbury report does not much address. Directors need to know about the business the firm is in to be both effective and independent but such knowledge and experience can be a double-edged sword. The Global Financial Crisis demonstrated this. Many banks, for example, were seen as having too few Board members with industry experience but others perhaps had too many, or too many retirees with experience that was not current, as at Lehman Brothers where four out of ten Board members were over 75 years of age and only one had current market experience. Yet Northern Rock had two board members with banking experience and seven out of thirteen Bear Stearns directors had a banking background and both institutions failed massively (Kirkpatrick 2009). How much experience a director should have, and of what type, is not entirely clear from a governance perspective.

The nature of actual Board and Board committee meeting process is also very important. Evidence from the Global Financial Crisis is cited of a sample of eleven European banks with risk committees in which half staffed their committees with non-executive directors but that in such cases the Chief Executive Officer (CEO), the CFO and the Chief Research Officer (CRO) were always in attendance and are reported to have played a major role in the committee's deliberations, quite probably biasing them (Kirkpatrick 2009).

This theme of Board composition and independence from the CEO and other top management recurs in the academic literature. An analysis of five major corporate failures in Australia in 2001 reveals that the boards at the failed companies generally had a below average number of independent directors with over-representations of founders and family members of founders, audit firm personnel and large shareholders. Similar patterns were found on many key Board committees, especially audit, where oft-times former audit personnel served (Watts 2002).

The broad empirical literature echoes some of these findings but is also more tentative. One review of the literature noted that the US evidence indicates that higher proportions of outside directors are not associated with superior firm performance, but are associated with better decisions concerning such issues as acquisitions, executive compensation, and CEO turnover, while board size is inversely related to both general firm performance and the quality of decision-making. International experience indicates that boards with more outside members are more likely to dismiss CEOs (Denis and McConnell 2003).

The Enron collapse in the US put a harsh spotlight on management capture of Boards in that country. The legislation passed afterwards, colloquially referred to as the Sarbanes-Oxley Act (SOX) after the names of its legislative sponsors, mandated many different things but Board independence was a key aspect, including a definition of independence now enshrined in US federal law and a requirement that key Board committees such as Compensation be entirely filled with independent members. Interestingly, though, this act did not prescribe a separation between Chair and CEO roles nor any limits on Board size (Jackson 2010), deviating from UK practice.

Indeed, the role and composition of the Board of Directors has been a long standing concern of both academics and policy-makers and one subject to its own cycles. In the US outside directors tended to be very rare decades ago, constituting 25% of all board members up to and through the 1970s, with very loose definitions of independence focusing largely on whether members were currently engaged by the firm, not concerned with past associations. Management-dominated firms were the norm in the US until the 1980s when hostile takeovers and leveraged buyouts shook up the corporate order and ended what had been referred to as 'managerial capitalism' (Jackson 2010). Yet failures and scandals have been recurrent both when Board independence was an aberration and now that it is an accepted ideal (if perhaps honoured more in the breach practically than otherwise).

Of equal interest has been the structure of shareholdings and the activism of shareholders. Most analyses contrast the US and UK patterns of generally more diffuse shareholdings with continental European and Asian patterns of block shareholders who have large holdings. Banks in particular have, in the past, held large share positions in many companies in parts of Europe and Asia, especially Japan and Germany. Which system is 'better' for corporate governance is a question that the literature has spent a lot of time on.

The evidence and arguments about the beneficence or otherwise of block shareholding have been mixed and have changed over time. Roe (2005) has argued that diffuse ownership in the US leads to crisis because it allows more concentration of power in the hands of managers because shareholder power is spread out too weakly across many holders. (Roe additionally argues that the problem is exacerbated by weak American regulatory structures that allow for what some call 'regulatory arbitrage' of firms playing one agency off another in a decentralised regulation space.)

Roe's thinking flows from a strain of thought that holds that concentrated ownership is better for governance because large shareholders are more effective and engaged monitors of both the Board and of corporate managers than small shareholders who have little incentive and ability to oversee manager performance. But of course who monitors the monitors? Equally possible is that large shareholders will try to extract value from smaller shareholders and will do so by manipulating management or perhaps being manipulated and 'captured' by management. There is the additional complication that Board members 'independent' of firm management may also need to be independent from the large shareholders as well to be genuine objective outsiders seeking to maximise total shareholder wealth (Becht et al. 2005).

Evidence on large shareholdings and firm value is unclear. This includes evidence on specific firm holdings by entities such as banks. There have been times when one 'system' seems to be doing particularly well macroeconomically and observers then ascribe such performance to broad corporate characteristics such as concentrated ownership. So when Japan seemed to be a dominant economy in the 1980s many attributed this success to its predominance of block shareholding and closely knit manager-shareholder relationships. A similar fad focused on European countries such as Germany, which has broadly similar characteristics, with banks playing a prominent ownership role. But of course as countries fade so do the reputations of their governance systems. Even diffuse ownership countries such as the US and the UK have witnessed changes in shareholding concentrations, and, perhaps as importantly, shareholder activism, as with the rise of pension fund investors who accumulate significant ownership blocs and are more willing to vote their shares contrary to management and ally with other significant holders to do so. Yet here too corporate governance problems ebb and flow and do not seem to abate in any significant degree overall (Becht et al. 2005).

More micro-evidence is not particularly conclusive either. There is little strong linkage between blockholdings and observed market value of firms, though there is some evidence, in the US, of blockholdings and exertions of private control and capture of private benefit. International evidence reveals that concentrated ownership structures are more typical of ownership structures around the world than those of large, publicly-traded US and UK firms. Yet even blockholding is not monolithic. Blocks of shares vary in their character-istics, including the proportion of total shares held, the types of holders (e.g. other corporations, families, governments etc.), the amount of corporate value represented by the shares held, and so forth. Bank block holdings in particular have varying effects on firm value. The broad takeaway is that concentrated ownership most often has a positive effect on firm value but there are many exceptions and nuances (Denis and McConnell 2003).

It should be noted that most of these studies focus primarily on blockholdings and firm value which is an important but limited measure of corporate governance and outcomes. It is also true that cross-holdings and share structure are important to actual control. 'Pryamided' structures in which one entity owns 51% of another, which owns 51% or yet another etc. can result in corporate control to a degree much larger than a mere ownership share might suggest as can special shares with greater voting rights than ordinary shares. And entities that own shares in each other, resulting in interlocking boards, can also be more powerful than their ownership shares suggest (Denis and McConnell 2003). Thus even though one company might appear to have 'concentrated' ownership and another one 'diffuse' ownership, actual control exerted by specific shareholders might actually be quite different. This is a general pitfall with summary prescriptions for governance based on summary measures of firm characteristics.

Executive compensation has been a major concern especially since the Enron collapse and then the Global Financial Crisis in which both the size of management packages and their link to share price and the attendant manipulations of those prices by managers loomed very large. It is very clear that pay linked to share price has grown prodigiously in the US especially. At their peak in 2001, stock options accounted for over 50% of the pay of CEOs of major United States firms (Rajagopalan and Zhang 2009: 548).

The OECD notes that remuneration and incentive systems have helped make financial institutions more sensitive to shocks by causing unsustainable balance sheet positions and incentivising short-term thinking and excessive risk-taking. One study of European banks is cited in which, in 2006, fixed salary accounted for 24% of CEO remuneration, annual cash bonuses for 36% and long-term incentive awards for only 40%; which is better than one study of six US financial institutions finding that top executive salaries averaged only 4–6% of total compensation as long-term incentives with stock related compensation (and especially stock options in two cases) hovering at very high levels. In this case incentive problems in remuneration ran from top management down to sales and trading function levels (Kirkpatrick 2009: 12–14).

The general thinking on incentives tends to follow standard Governance Theory: tie pay to company performance, with a mix of emphasis on short-term share value and longer-term performance overall. This supposedly will align Principal and Agent motivations. But what such a pay package actually looks like is, as should already be obvious, not easy to nail down. The evidence and theory suggests, first, that there are limits to how much of a firm managers should actually own before it starts being able to exert too much influence on its own behalf. A 1999 study of inside ownership in the UK finds entrenchment effects of managerial ownership begin to dominate the Principal–Agent alignment incentives when management ownership is 12%, considerably higher than the 5% threshold found in a US study (Denis and McConnell 2003). In other words if managers own too much of a company, without outright control of it, they may be in position to extract value from other owners by using their management control in combination with their large shareholding power.

This is something of an exceptional situation, however, especially in the UK and US. More general US evidence seems to support a general correlation between firm performance and the level and nature of CEO pay. Some recent studies suggest CEO pay is actually not as 'excessive' (suggesting management capture of the firm), or rising as fast as some analysts and the general discourse suggests, which may indicate an ebbing of compensation conditions that many felt help bring on the financial collapse in 2008 (Conyon 2014; Kaplan 2012). However executive pay is not always easy to measure and cause and effect are not always clear, e.g. a growing firm may simply pay executives more, regardless of how well the CEO is actually performing and contingent compensation schemes such as share options can sometimes be hard to value ex ante. UK evidence finds a similarly positive relationship between pay and performance but does not find the association statistically significant. The study author in that case suggests that this may indicate that post-Cadbury report reforms seeking to tie pay more closely to performance in that country may not have been totally successful (Ozkan 2011).

Of course executives often have substantial influence over their own compensation, and have used this power in some instances to game the system to their own advantage. Some studies have shown the size of share options outstanding are closely related to the prevalence of earnings restatements, while another study confirms that while US CEO pay has moved from being unlinked to sharemarket capitalisation, as it was during the 1950s and 1960s, to being closely linked with it now, this has not increased the relative sensitivity of pay to performance, especially because much of the performance payment pay has been in the form of share options – something that leaves a lot of discretion to management to exercise or not. There also seems to be variability in the relationship between pay for performance depending upon firm size and market sentiment (Jackson 2010). While the logic behind Principal–Agent alignment through compensation seems sound, the reality is not as easy to tease out and hard-and-fast rules are difficult to formulate.

The Enron debacle in particular showed the importance of governance 'gatekeepers', a topic that the literature had not paid much attention to up until then. In the Enron case the role of independent auditors in perpetrating malfeasance was highlighted when Enron's auditor, Arthur Andersen, then highly respected, was shown to be complicit in the company's fraudulent activities and was itself shut down shortly after the Enron bankruptcy. After the GFC the role of another gatekeeper, the credit ratings agencies, was found to be wanting as many banks and investment firms were given the highest ratings shortly before going bust or encountering major problems (Coffee 2011).

Traditionally, gatekeepers such as accountants, auditors and corporate lawyers were thought of as being sufficiently based in their respective professional ethos as to be independent enough to be considered unlikely to sacrifice their reputation for the benefit of any single client. But changes in the professions as they became deregulated and as law and auditing firms in particular became more consolidated and aggressively commercialised began to shift both perception and reality as incidents of conflicts of interest grew. The quality of audits declined in tandem with an increase of non-audit services by auditing firms beginning in the 1990s. Perhaps not coincidentally the number of earnings restatements issued by listed corporations more than tripled (Jackson 2010; Coffee 2006). And then, of course, Enron. And after that, the Global Financial Crisis. Those crises have driven various legislative reforms governing gatekeepers. It remains to be seen how effective these have been.

The issue of gatekeepers is one that straddles the boundary between internal and external firm governance. Researchers have increasingly focused on the systemic context within which a firm operates and how this affects and is affected by what happens within firm boundaries. Denis and McConnell (2003) refer to this as 'second generation' corporate governance research. Whereas the 'first generation' focused on the firm in isolation, this second wave takes a more holistic view.

A significant strain might be termed 'law and finance', after the seminal article of the same title by LaPorta, Lopez-de-Silanes, Shleifer and Vishny (LLSV) (1998). This view posits that the system of law under which a company operates is the well from which much corporate governance structure and functioning flows. The varied details of this literature will not be covered in any detail here, but the basic thrust is that common law countries lead to different optimal internal governance procedures and conditions than civil law systems. For example, common law countries generally have better investor legal protections than civil law countries and so concentrated shareholdings may make more sense in firms in the latter countries than in the former, and this can explain observed shareholding patterns (Denis and McConnell 2003).

The strength of enforcement of laws also has been observed to affect corporate governance outcomes and practices. And social norms are very important as well (and perhaps linked to enforcement policies). Coffee (2001), for example, suggests that strong egalitarian social norms in Scandinavia may discourage expropriation of value from minority investors and that such norms there may allow for weak laws and enforcement, and suggesting the reverse for countries where norms are weak, which may be why US laws are so prescriptive and weak enforcement there is so often associated with scandal. This general pattern seems to have been generally confirmed by later research (Boytsun et al. 2011).

Coffee (1998) claims corporate governance research is becoming more evolutionary in its approach to account for all these multiple causes and effects. In other words, there are now multiple theoretical approaches in which ideas about corporate form and function and environment interact with each other in ways similar to the way species interact in an ecosystem. So atomistic neoclassical ideas about firm governance being driven purely by a competitive marketplace can coexist with more institutionally oriented ideas to create a productive and dynamic system of ideas rather than more Kuhnian ideas of one paradigm supplanting another, though that can happen too.

Coffee proffers two research questions that he sees as paramount: '(1) Which system of corporate governance is superior?, and (2) Which set of forces – economic or political – are likely to prove more powerful?' (1998: 643). Coffee holds that corporate governance results from a combination of internal firm design choices and social, legal and political context that both limits and channels those choices. 'Accidents' of historical circumstance, and 'path dependence', are very important as well to determing how general firm governance manifests and evolves.

An example of a more neoclassical approach to governance form, function and evolution can be found in the 'market for corporate control'. This term was coined by Manne (1965) and refers to the notion that optimal governance is directly shaped by the market itself in which poorly governed companies will either fail or have their management forced out by those with capital and know-how to take over the firm and put it under superior direction. This sort of thinking was behind much of the hostile takeover movement in the US and, to a lesser degree, the UK, in which financiers would agglomerate pools of capital and employ leverage to take over firms, force out incumbent managers, and at times strip out assets before selling out (or more hopefully, cut deadwood and reform the company into a competitive enterprise). This 1980s and 1990s phenomenon was helped along by liberalisation in capital markets in New York and London and an associated relaxation of national anti-trust and other corporate public regulation.

The effectiveness of this market process is debatable. Some inefficient companies were certainly reformed in past waves of hostile takeovers and consolidations, but there are many examples where such takeovers resulted in governance failures and questionable practices that reduced rather than increased performance. In the US this trend was broken by enactment of many anti-takeover provisions in state and federal law and corporate policy changes such as 'poison pills' (which required large payments to incumbent shareholders in the case of a merger or acquisition being enacted) and 'golden parachutes' (which required large payouts to ousted managers) (Becht et al. 2005). Still, takeovers, now much less hostile, have been and remain far more common in the US than many other countries, especially those with more concentrated shareholdings, which does suggest that diffuse American holdings perhaps do rely more on market dynamics to shape corporate governance (Denis and McConnell 2003). And certainly competitive markets in the buying and selling of firms are good for winnowing out poor management.

This review is, of course, far from complete and should not be read as suggesting settled knowledge. It has already been indicated that dominant research in the field has moved from first generation to second generation and towards more varied models of cause and effect. The world that is being studied is also subject to rapid change, especially an increasingly globalised world which has spawned an large literature on international business specifically (Casson 2013; Dunning 2013). The main point to be emphasised here is that there is nonetheless an underlying structure of thought that seems to flow in fairly well-defined channels of Principal, Agent and alignment of the two that would be familiar to neoclassical thinkers.

Some standard policy solutions

The solutions to corporate problems enshrined in legislation fairly closely follow the ideas presented in the literature. This can be seen in major acts passed in the UK and the US especially in response to major failures in the 1990s and 2000s. (Policy responses to the Global Financial Crisis in these countries have tended to be more focused on systemic risk and practices in the financial sector in particular and thus will be less of a focus here, though discussed as relevant.)

Jackson (2010: 36) mentions that by 2000:

> most of the key pillars in the U.S. 'model' of corporate governance were in place, and conventional wisdom began to see these elements as a normative benchmark for 'good' corporate governance practices around the world. Shareholder engagement would be supplied by active institutional investors.

Boards would be increasingly independent and rewarded through long-term equity based incentives linked to share price performance. The flow of information from the board was certified by outside gatekeepers, such as auditors and accountants. Taken together, these elements also served as a foundation for an effective market for corporate control.

Then Enron occurred, in the midst of widespread accounting irregularity overall, and this model now seemed in need of repair. In fact, rather than reinforcing good governance, the various pillars seemed to be collapsing in on each other in a race to the bottom rather than upholding a temple of Olympian governance strength. Now it seemed that Boards were routinely captured by their executives, executives then captured the gatekeepers, and shareholders suspended disbelief as they received large but unsustainable paper gains in their shareholdings. The system had seemed to be well-grounded in theory, relying on the mechanisms of market incentives (including a supposedly active market for corporate control), disclosure, and independence at the Board level to provide checks and balances between firm governance and market dynamics, and an overarching network of professionals to keep everyone honest (Jackson 2010). Yet the system did not seem to work, suggesting a need for a fundamental rethink.

The American legislative response to Enron was contained in the Sarbanes-Oxley Act , referred to as 'SOX' for short. A major element of SOX was reforming the audit process. This was probably the most innovative part of SOX in that before then US regulation did not much address gatekeepers at all, and auditing firms in particular. Now auditors are banned from receiving non-audit fees and subject to regulation and oversight by a new agency called the Public Company Accounting Oversight Board (PCAOB). A company board's audit committee is supposed to oversee firm-auditor relationships and must be composed entirely of independent directors (Jackson 2010: 39). Additionally lead accounting audit partners must rotate every five years. SOX also set new requirements for firm internal control systems, requiring a firm CEO and CFO to attest to the effectiveness of those controls; report deficiencies to firm auditors and the board audit committee; and requiring management to report on the effectiveness of internal controls (Becht et al. 2005).

To limit CEO incentives to manipulate earnings, SOX requires CEOs to reimburse any contingent payments they received based on past overstated earnings and companies are now forbidden to extend loans to CEOs that are repayable in company shares. This last reform was inspired particularly by Worldcom's massive loans to its CEO Bernie Ebbers who later resigned in disgrace and was then charged and convicted in US federal court. Greater disclosure of off-balance sheet transactions were also mandated. An interesting provision is the greater protections given by SOX to internal firm whistle-blowers, of which one played a key role in exposing the problems at Enron (Becht et al. 2005).

Although SOX had more of a focus on gatekeepers and internal firm controls, there was a bit of attention paid to the composition and focus of Boards. These provisions were taken up by the New York Stock Exchange (NYSE) (and the NASDAQ stock exchange which undertook parallel reforms in their listing requirements in 2002), mandating that listed firms have a majority of independent directors, with Compensation and Nominating committees consisting entirely of independent directors (though NASDAQ requirements are a bit more flexible). SOX itself contains a new definition of an "independent" director as someone who may not "accept any consulting, advisory, or other compensatory fee from the issuer; or be a person affiliated with the issuer or any subsidiary thereof" (SOX Article 301) and the US share exchanges follow this definition (Jackson 2010: 42).

However, post-Enron reforms have not introduced any rules on board size or separation of the CEO and Chair positions. And in many ways SOX is a very incremental bill, firmly grounded in the 'consensus' view of good corporate governance and remaining committed to the pillars of the model in place that existed pre-Enron. Its major departure is a focus on gatekeepers, previously rather neglected in policy, though with many noting alarming trends in that arena years before the scandals early in this current century. But the basic structure of the current governance model is not subject to any substantial revision. Initial rules and regulations implementing the law were widely attacked as being overly costly to comply with though these have since been revised and simplified (Jackson 2010: 40). In sum SOX is far from a fundamental rethink, instead taking the existing system and imposing new external governmental mandates on top of it.

It should be noted that SOX has had a profound influence on foreign companies, partly through indirect example and partly because of the listing rule changes of the NYSE or NASDAQ. Foreign firms listed on a US stock exchange, and foreign subsidiaries of US firms, are hence subject to SOX requirements. Some firms have chosen to deregister from US exchanges, especially smaller ones, but larger ones have mostly complied (Jackson 2010: 46–47).

And what of the US legislative response to the even bigger crisis that would come a mere six years after Enron? In some ways the response was huge in terms of government bank bailouts, massive infusions of monetary resources by the central bank and long-term maintenance of close to zero-percent interest rates, and substantial new regulations of the financial sector.

But the legislative response with respect to general corporate governance was actually weaker than SOX. The Dodd-Frank Act (the colloquial name also after the names of its US Congressional co-sponsors) enacted in 2010, imposed new oversight over a previously neglected gatekeeper, that of the credit ratings agencies (consisting primarily the big three US firms of Standard and Poor's, Moody's and Fitch). These firms were supposed to give independent and unbiased ratings of securities risk but were glaringly caught out by giving good ratings to firms that sometimes mere months later failed. Dodd-Frank created a new Office of Credit Ratings to watch over Nationally Recognized Statistical Ratings Organizations (NRSRO) that rate the financial worthiness of securities and creating a notional liability for 'reckless' ratings (Docking, 2012: 24). The law's major focus was, however, on the operations of financial institutions, some policies of the US Federal Reserve Bank, and the general handling of systemic risk in the financial system. While very important, especially to financial services firms, this is not a general corporate governance reform bill.

There are parts of the Act, however, that do deal specifically with executive compensation. Corporate shareholders are now given a statutory right to a non-binding vote on executive pay and golden parachutes. The Securities and Exchange Commission (SEC) which regulates publicly listed American firms now has authority to grant shareholders proxy access to nominate directors. Compensation committees of boards of companies listed on a US share exchange are now required to have these committees consist only of independent directors and now have authority to hire independent compensation consultants. Public companies must also have policies to claw back any executive compensation based on inaccurate financial statements that don't comply with accounting standards (US Senate 2010).

Still, the overall US response to the Global Financial Crisis was to treat it as mostly a finance sector crisis and not a more general corporate governance crisis. Even though there were individual governance failures as great as there were at Enron, these were mostly confined to financial intermediaries. And the systemic issues were much broader. Whether this is an entirely appropriate and effective response remains to be seen. It is clear though that SOX, which affected all major companies, did not seem to brake the many abuses that led to Global Financial Crisis.

The other major Anglophone country considered here is the UK. Its big corporate governance crises pre-dated Enron by a decade and its reforms were strongly shaped by the influential Cadbury Commission, already mentioned. A number of reports and commissions followed: the Greenbury Report (1995) focused on executive remuneration, and the Hampel Committee (1998), which reviewed the corporate governance recommendations in force in the UK at that time. The recommendations of the Turnbull Report (1999) focused on internal controls and risk (Mallin et al. 2005).

Much of this was incorporated into the Combined Code in 1998, which contained the governance requirements for companies listed on the London stock exchange. It was revised in 2003 and then replaced by the UK Corporate Governance Code, overseen by the Financial Reporting Council, which itself has been revised to account for the events of the Global Financial Crisis. The Code was based on a 'comply or explain' model in which non-compliant companies had to explain why they chose not to comply. Evidence shows that more than half of the largest UK nonfinancial companies complied fully and only around 10% failed to comply with even a single provision, though the non-complying firms often explained themselves poorly or not all in 1 out of 5 non-compliant cases (Arcot et al. 2010). Despite this, the approach was thought to be superior to mandate models like SOX because it allowed for creativity and flexibility by individual companies. Or so the theory goes.

The Combined Code states that there should be an effective board and calls for a separation of the roles of Chair and CEO. There is to be a balance of executive and non-executive directors (and in particular independent non-executive directors), and a formal, rigorous and transparent procedure for the appointment of new directors. Information should be provided to the board in a timely manner and all directors should regularly update their skills and knowledge. Board performance, at the general, committee, and individual levels, should be formally and rigorously evaluated and all directors should stand for regular re-election intervals, unless removed for poor performance. The Combined Code states that "remuneration should be sufficient to attract, retain and motivate directors of the quality required to run the company successfully" and that the board should establish an audit committee of independent non-executive directors. The Combined Code not only addresses companies and boards but also recommends that institutional investors should have a dialogue with companies and are exhorted to make considered use of their votes (Mallin et al. 2005).

The successor UK Corporate Governance Code carries forward many of these principles, including the 'comply or explain' approach. It adds provisions stating that performance-related pay should be aligned to long-term company interests and risk management; that all directors of FTSE 350 companies should be put forward for re-election every year; establishes new principles on the leadership of the chairman and the responsibility of the non-executive directors to provide constructive challenge to management; and also puts forward new principles on the composition and selection of the board, including the need to appoint members on merit, against objective criteria, and with due regard for the benefits of diversity, including gender diversity. Board chairs of FTSE 350 firms are encouraged to hold regular development reviews with each director and have externally facilitated board effectiveness reviews at least every three years. And boards are encouraged to consider the benefits of diversity across all dimensions so as to try to ensure a well-balanced board and avoid 'group think' (Financial Reporting Council 2014).

Sitting atop this is the Companies Act of 2006. This Act contains many shareholder engagement provisions including the right to call a shareholder meeting with Directors, to have a statement of proposed solution to problems distributed to members and to have long-term service contracts approved by shareholders. Many of these rights existed before but were codified and strengthened by the Act (National Archives (UK), 2014a).

After the Global Financial Crisis, the Financial Reporting Council published the Stewardship Code in 2010 and revised it in 2012. This too addresses shareholder rights and responsibilities, especially those of institutional shareholders who are encouraged to state how they will satisfy their stewardship responsibilities, manage their conflicts of interest, and collaborate with other investors on monitoring of management. The contents of this Code echoes much of what was contained in a voluntary Institutional Shareholder's Committee (ISC) statement on the 'Responsibilities of Institutional Shareholders in the UK,' which actually predated the Cadbury Commission (Roach 2011).

Unlike the US the UK has generally relied on the 'soft law' approach of 'comply or explain', which using Coffee's rubric might suggest the greater strength of social norms there. The focus on institutional investors is an outgrowth of greater concentration of shareholdings in the UK, though it remains more diffuse in that country than in many of its Continental counterparts.

The Global Financial Crisis did however raise questions how about effective a soft law approach actually is and the new UK 'say on pay' legislation is a notable departure from it because it is legally binding, with sanctions possible for non-compliance in appropriate circumstances. Formally known as the Enterprise and Regulatory Reform Act – 2013, this legislation enables company shareholders to have a binding vote on director pay and puts on them an obligation to enhance remuneration policy every three years. Director pay must either adhere to the approved policy or else be directly approved by the shareholders. The legislation only applies to directors of listed companies based in the UK, though, not to overseas companies listed on the UK sharemarket (National Archives (UK) 2014b).

The Large and Medium-sized Companies and Groups (Accounts and Reports) (Amendment) Regulations – 2013 is another 'hard law' act that outlines reporting requirements for companies' future remuneration policies and Annual Reports with fairly robust and specific disclosure requirements, specifically on company justification and process for deciding on and setting remuneration level for directors. A company must also show how the components of a director's remuneration back up the company's immediate and future plans (National Archives (UK) 2014c).

As in the US the Global Financial Crisis inspired a lot of legislation but most of it was focused on the finance sector and practices there. Corporate governance policy changes were made but they were relatively small given the crisis, in largely incremental ways that built off an already existing structure.

UK corporate governance legislation differs from the US in a number of ways, however. The UK focus on soft law is one difference already noted, but one that may be slowly shifting towards the US hard mandates philosophy. The UK governance approach can also be seen to at least implicitly incorporate some behavioural economics insights, at least mildly. The focus on board and shareholder group dynamics and process and social networks has a clear parallel to the literature on peer and group influences. The emphasis on board diversity is not just about social equity but about ameliorating some of the well-known anomalies of human decision-making.

And, in fact UK policy-makers have explicitly incorporated some findings of behavioural economics in other arenas. Prime Minister David Cameron established a Behavioural Insights Team in the Cabinet Office (which is called the 'Nudge Unit'), having Richard Thaler as an official (unpaid) advisor. (In the US, Cass Sunstein serves as Barack Obama's regulation 'tsar' [Health Affairs Blog 2011]). But in the corporate governance arena there is still more of a flavour rather than a large paradigm shift.

Incorporating macroeconomic insights

This chapter will finish by touching upon a separate strain of inquiry that focuses on the observed persistent fact of extreme macrcoeconomic cycles in developed countries once every one or two generations. One of the core notions of neoclassical Economic Theory and its governance offspring is that the sum of the parts is equal to the whole. In other words, one can describe the collective of the firm as simply the collection of the individual behaviours of Agents and Principals who come together to form its nexus. However human beings are clearly affected by their fellows and what a group does, even a small one, is often far different than what the individuals would do in isolation. These collective effects, whether driven by sociality or something else, can have a significant impact and need to be accounted for in corporate governance settings.

There is both a microeconomic and a macroeconomic scale for this. Behavioural economics is all about the microeconomics in that it is abstracts away from the larger economic cycles of boom, bust and stasis and focuses on individual actors with macroeconomic conditions assumed away. However the shape of the overall economy affects and is affected by individual decisions. There is real scope to integrate these issues into corporate governance.

The evolution of macroeconomics as a field is obviously far beyond the scope of this book. But prior to the Great Depression Anglo–American economists thought that one could explain the macro-economy solely through a microeconomic model. The Depression, which persisted despite massive price deflation that was supposed to re-equilibrate the economy back to full employment by lowering wages enough to make workers attractive to hire again and capital cheap enough to deploy again, made people rethink the economic models of the time. John Maynard Keynes was the most influential of these thinkers, giving birth to a whole school of 'Keynesianism' which often departed from his premises despite taking on his name (Barber 2010).

Keynes' theory contains quite a few 'psychological' notions that are reminiscent of behavioural economics today. The macroeconomic dimension need not concern us here. But some of Keynes' observations about actor behaviour and action are relevant. In particular Keynes argues that there is no sound objective basis in the present for calculating probabilities of business success on which to make investment decisions (because of basic uncertainty about the future, which becomes clear only with the passage of time). This leads to the formation of fragile expectations about the future and prices of capital assets in the present based on tenuous perceptions that are therefore subject to sudden and violent change.

Keynes also points to the importance of 'mass sentiment' in the formation of expectations, i.e. the notion that what everyone else thinks affects what an individual thinks. And he posited the phenomenon of 'money illusion' which is the idea that at least for some period of time, often very long periods, people confuse nominal income with real income, basing their decisions on the monetary prices in the present without fully accounting for inflation, another economic variable that also often becomes clear to actors only after a significant lag. Finally, and most famously, Keynes noted that, in the 'long run', 'real' economic asset values and expected or perceived asset values must align but that this could be a very long time period indeed in human terms, captured in the famous epigram:

'[I]n the long run we are all dead' (Keen 1995: 608–609). The observations about money illusion and the difference between short-term and long-term decision-making have in fact been carried over into current behavioural economics.

Much of Keynes' psychology was ad hoc and with no particular specification of how expectation formation actually occurred. Here is where Hyman Minsky came in decades later. He actually uses the term 'bounded rationality' in some of his writings, contrasting this to the 'rational expectations' present in many neo-classically based macroeconomic treatises that arose in the 1970s and which now constitute the basis of a full-blown intellectual program to re-integrate micro-economics and macroeconomics into a renewed and revised neoclassical paradigm.

Minsky claims that individual mental models cannot capture the 'deep uncertainty of decentralised systems in which a myriad of independent agents make decisions whose impacts are aggregated into outcomes that emerge over a range of tomorrows' (Minsky 1996: 7). Rational expectations, by contrast, assumes a common understanding of reality across agents, based on objective metrics. In actual fact, Minsky claims, agents have individual understandings of reality that often differ from one another, sometimes in significant ways, and that depart from objectivity which itself may be in formation and known with clarity often quite some time later. Human expectation models are thus at best 'provisional' and so individual views about the future cannot simply be summed up to arrive at a consensus forecast, which is the basis of rational expectations.

Minsky's major contribution, and the one most relevant for the purposes here, was his tying of the financial cycle to both this premise of human frailty and human sociality (though he does not actually use this term). Given provisional expectations that are largely subjective to begin with he explored the way in which those expectations might be formed, something Keynes only hinted at. Minsky argued that prices of most end-consumer commodities sold by business are set by a mark up on prime costs which means that the initial prices of assets which produce these commodities, directly or indirectly, are based on initial estimates of future cash flows, not on the original cost of production or the true economic marginal cost. Expectations about asset prices thus vary over, and according to, the financial cycle because that cycle and the general economic environment affect estimates of future cash flows. The state of these expectations in turn influences the economic cycle by stimulating human moods of optimism and pessimism on a societal scale. In the long-term asset prices must equilibrate with fundamental asset costs (Minsky is certainly no post-modernist in this respect) but, as Keynes pointed out, that can be a very long time indeed. Until then, mass psychology plays a critical role in responding to and then affecting the larger economy (Keen 1995: 610).

As far as dynamics goes, Minsky starts his theory with actors at a point when the economy is doing well but with the memory of a past financial crash still in place. Borrowing and lending is conservative because risk premiums on lending are very high as people are still very sensitive to the trauma of past systemic losses. However the combination of a good economy and conservative finance means that most financed projects succeed.

At some point expectations of investment success as a matter of course begin to rise and corresponding risk premia and risk aversion on the part of businesses and investors begin to fall. At first this can be seen as an adjustment to the underlying reality that economic conditions are in fact favourable and the overabundance of caution is whittled away. But while a neoclassical model would stop at a equilibrium where the marginal cost of capital is equal to its marginal return, the Minsky model does not stop there. For the marginal costs and benefits that business uses to estimate asset prices and that lenders use to assess credit risk are still based on expectations and thus subject to individual psychology which is in turn subject to mass psychology. So an investment boom begins to build, bidding up asset prices and attracting more and more external capital seeking returns (and worrying less about risk), something Minsky calls the 'euphoric economy'.

The seeds of the next bust, however, are built into this boom. Firms become more leveraged as they perceive that risks are lower than they actually are and they expand more than actual risk-reward tradeoffs, which are not correctly perceived, would suggest. Meanwhile, financial intermediaries lower credit standards in their lending. Both of these developments reduce firm liquidity and make firms more susceptible to increases in interest rates because everyone in the system has increased their borrowing and debt service costs as a percentage of total income have risen to unsustainable levels. The financial sector, meanwhile, has built up a portfolio of loans that gets increasingly shaky and sensitive to external shocks or even small changes that can lead to a rise in interest rates. Also a new actor (who could be an individual working within existing institutions or setting up a new institution), the 'Ponzi financier', arises, who engages in purely speculative investment based on leverage and asset flipping based on rising asset prices in the context of low interest rates. The finance sector, both traditional and 'Ponzi' both encourage purely speculative investment and an asset boom.

There is, of course, a choke point being set up for a liquidity squeeze once cost of capital increases even slightly. This rise comes soon as demand for credit simply outpaces supply and cost of money cannot help but rise eventually. It is sometimes brought on early by some external event such as a bank failure. Either way the squeeze begins when both firms and Ponzi financiers find themselves having to sell assets to meet financing costs. This begins to slow or reverse the rise in asset prices which lowers the value of collateral that has been put forward to secure loans, resulting in calls for new collateral or immediate repayment of loan amounts. Liquidity now becomes increasingly prized over illiquid capital that is falling in price and at some point the asset bubble bursts and the boom becomes a slump. To re-equilibrate asset prices back into harmony with their long lost fundamentals either asset price deflation must occur or current price inflation. With high inflation stagflation occurs – growth is reduced and price inflation is high – but at least bankruptcy is limited since borrower liabilities are falling in real terms. At least a big bust is avoided, which will not be the case when there is asset price deflation that drives institutions into insolvency and bankruptcy (Keen 1995: 611–613; Minsky 1977, 1984).

Minksy then puts forward something he calls the 'financial instability hypothesis', which claims that modern capitalist systems will have inevitable boom and busts. Minsky's focus is on how to solve the macroeconomic problem and his work has been highly influential in current understanding of the Global Financial Crisis and monetary policy responses to that crisis in which the US central bank, the Fed, has kept interest rates extremely low and sought to foster moderate price inflation to avoid the disastrous price deflation of the 1930s (Minsky 1995). In fact although the US Federal Reserve Bank is not legally allowed to take ownership positions in failing financial intermediaries, it did, in conjunction with the US federal government, effectively do just that after the latest crisis, especially through 'Quantitative Easing' (QE) in which huge portions of private but largely worthless assets were brought on to the Bank's balance sheet, many of which still remain there. This is a manoeuvre adapted from Minsky's crisis playbook. Indeed Minsky argued twenty years ago that the Federal Reserve Bank will come to realise that its proper role is not to maintain stable prices but stable financing conditions which is in fact what it has come to do since the Global Financial Crisis, as have other major central banks around the world (Minsky 1995: 92).

However, the important point for this discussion is the role of mass psychology that Minsky develops and the close link between financial market changes and corporate organisational and related governance changes that he identifies. General business conditions can and do affect business decisions made within firms at critical points and these must be accounted for by policy-makers and theorists.

This shows how closely some 'macro' and 'micro' streams of thought are tracking one another now and how relevant some of the macroeconomic literature findings are for policy responses to corporate governance and for corporate governance design more generally. Indeed, economists George Akerlof and Robert Shiller wrote a 2009 book that can be seen as a macroeconomic application of behavioural economics, using a catalog of 'animal spirits' and how these affect overall economic process and performance (Akerlof and Shiller 2009).

Meanwhile, the strong links between private governance decisions and legislative, regulatory, legal and social environment that the so-called 'second generation' of corporate governance empirical research is, in many ways, a 'micro' counterpart to this macroeconomic project. All of which shows that the firm is, indeed, a 'nexus', a whole that is greater than the sum of parts rather than an identity with it as the neoclassical theory suggests. A key task is to try to pull these disparate strands into some kind of useful framework. This will be the subject of the next chapter.

5 Towards a behavioural governance framework

The mainstream theoretical understanding of corporate governance relies on a neoclassical economic understanding of the firm in a world of atomistic, self-seeking, rational actors where the major problem to be addressed is a misalignment of Principal and Agent incentives. The standard solutions to these problems still dominate: getting compensation schemes 'right', making separation of Board and management clear, transparent and robust, improving internal firm deliberative processes, and keeping the whole process honest and disciplined with good gatekeepers and a market for corporate control in the background. Newer and broader theories do now emphasise the role of regulation and background legal systems as well as other institutions. But overall mainstream governance policy prescriptions and theorisation remain incremental, flowing through wider but still largely neoclassically constrained channels.

Still, the mainstream, even this expanded one, has been forced to reckon with two developments. One is the behavioural strain of economics which identifies empirically validated systematic and regular deviations of actors from the neoclassical model's predictions about how they are supposed to behave, and which has an older macroeconomic counterpart. The other perhaps more significant force is the empirical fact of repeated corporate failure and malfunction which persists despite best efforts and ideas to arrest it and which exhibits forms, such as overconfidence, myopia, and social pressure, that sometimes seem to fly in the face of the usual neoclassical operating assumptions. While some random variation in corporate function and malfunction are to be expected, the recurrent and severe cycles of governance blow-up suggest that existing theory and practice is missing something fundamental.

So some changes to the thinking on, and the prescriptions for, corporate governance are in order. The intellectual template most developed and yet argued here to be also the most conservative and hence most acceptable to mainstream discourse is behavioural economics. So this discussion will be organised along the same themes as in chapter three – modifications to rationality, maximisation, selfishness and atomism – and the focus will be on applying the findings of that literature to corporate governance reform specifically.

This chapter will also take a solutions-oriented approach. While there is still much to learn, there is a solid core of knowledge about human behaviour in the economic realm and ways of adjusting it for improved outcomes. So the generalisations presented in Chapter 3 will be applied and crystallised into possible suggested changes for corporate governance practice and presented in an over-arching framework. A discussion of more robust theory-building that takes into account other perspectives is presented in Chapter 6.

Behavioural problems and solutions: a recap

Table 5.1 provides a summary of the major heuristics, biases and errors that were presented in Chapter 3. Table 5.2 recapitulates the potential 'fixes' to adjust for these human quirks, as derived from the broad behavioural findings. Finally, Table 5.3 recapitulates the major themes of first- and second-generation corporate governance research in the economically inspired tradition, and which was discussed in more detail in Chapter 3.

Let's consider the implications of this for corporate governance. But first a nuance: the focus here is primarily on implications for Principals and Agents and not on other parties that feed into the nexus of the firm such as consumers or suppliers. Many if not most behavioural studies however focus on parties other than Principals and Agents, consumers especially. Therefore many of the existing findings will be adapted to Principals and Agents in the firm. It could be argued that these in particular are more sophisticated than the average consumer but as Kahneman and Tversky themselves noted in their original work, even sophisticated experts can be shown to make systematic human 'mistakes.' This is not to say that other parties are not equally important. But this is closest to the emphasis of most corporate governance research thus far along more traditional lines.

A common element: the human being

A simple way to think of a behavioural corporate governance framework is simple: just add the quirky human being into it. Then one can ask how this might appreciably change the predictions of theory and what sorts of safeguards might be applied.

In this case the neoclassical model is taken as a given but modified to introduce heuristics and biases. There are a lot of these so some sort of roadmap is useful to enter into this task. Table 5.4 is an attempt to do this. It is labelled as an inventory – that is, a checklist which can be used to organise an inquiry into either an individual firm or into firms more generally.

Table 5.1 Behavioural biases, errors and heuristics – deviations from:

Rationality	Maximisation	Self-interest	Atomism
The 'present bias' and the 'peanuts effect'	Time-inconsistent preferences	Voluntary public good provision	Public commitment effects
Anchoring	Endogenous preferences	Social norming	Social influence effects
'Framing effects'	Issues of self-control	Fairness reference effects	Authority and obedience
The 'overconfidence bias' and the 'curse of knowledge'	Intrinsic motivation	Unselfish game behaviour	Cross-cultural and cross-group effects
'Completeness bias'	Satiation		
The 'planning fallacy'	Loss aversion		
'Unrealistic optimism' ('Optimism bias')	Absolute versus relative changes		
'Choice/information overload'	Ill-defined or unstable preferences		
'Hindsight' and 'outcome biases' and the 'halo effect'	Goal-less behaviour		
'Self-serving bias', 'belief bias' and 'confirmation bias/ myside bias'	Reference-dependence		
'Salience'	'Status-quo bias'		
Feedback effects	'Endowment effects'		
Contextual effects	'Gestalt' effects'		
'Regression to the mean'	Complexity, ambiguity and lack of experience		
'Less is more fallacy'	Preference reversals		
Mood-altered judgement	Mental accounting and choice bracketing		
'Omission/commission bias'	Satisficing		
Pattern-seeking			
Representativeness bias			
Availability bias			
Prospect Theory			

Table 5.2 Potential 'fixes' to behavioural deviations

Solution	Deviations primarily addressed
Change default options	Rationality, Maximisation
Use present bias	Rationality
Limit and simplify options	Rationality
Strategically pick the form of incentives	Rationality, Self-interest, Maximisation
Encourage looking at things differently	Rationality, Maximisation
Use social forces	Atomism, Self-interest
Reframe things	Rationality
Structure decision support	Rationality, Maximisation
Utilise salience	Rationality, Maximisation
Imagine alternatives	Rationality, Atomism
Re-train	Rationality, Maximisation, Atomism
Re-design disclosure	Rationality
Provide cooling off periods	Rationality, Maximisation
Consider the opposite	Rationality, Maximisation, Atomism
Use decoys	Rationality
Employ pre-commitment devices	Maximisation
Practice, practice, practice	Rationality, Maximisation
Provide immediate feedback	Rationality, Maximisation, Atomism
Understand differences in people	Atomism, Self-interest, Maximisation
Use routines and algorithms in some instances	Maximisation, Rationality, Atomism

Table 5.3 Major themes of economistic corporate governance research

- Composition and independence of the Board of Directors
- Board of Directors structure
- Role of the CEO
- Structure and composition of shareholdings
- Executive compensation
- Independence and nature of 'gatekeepers'
- Legal and regulatory environment
- Social and other norms and institutions
- Strength of external market forces ('the market for corporate control'

Table 5.4 An inventory of potential behavioural effects on actors in the corporate nexus

	Rationality biases	Maximisation biases	Self-interest biases	Atomism biases
'Internal' nexus	– The 'present bias' – The 'peanuts effect'	– **Time–inconsistent preferences**	– Voluntary public good provision	– **Public commitment effects**
Owners (Principals)	– **Anchoring**	– Endogenous preferences	– **Social norming**	– **Social influence effects**
Shareholders	– **'Framing effects'**	– Issues of self-control	– **Fairness reference effects**	– **Authority and obedience**
– as a group	– **'Overconfidence bias' and the 'curse of knowledge'**	– **Intrinsic motivation**	– Unselfish game behaviour	– Cross-cultural and cross-group effects
– as individuals	– **'Completeness bias'**	– Satiation		
– composition	– **The 'planning fallacy'**	– **Loss aversion**		
– process	– **'Unrealistic optimism', ('Optimism bias')**	– **Absolute versus relative changes**		
Board of Directors	– **'Choice and information overload'**	– **Ill-defined or unstable preferences**		
– structure	– **'Hindsight' and 'outcome biases' and the 'halo effect'**	– Goal-less behaviour		
– process	– **'Self-serving bias', 'belief bias' and 'confirmation bias/myside bias'**	– **Reference-dependence**		
– individuals	– **'Salience'**	– **'Status-quo bias'**		
Agents (Management)	– Feedback effects	– **'Endowment effects'**		
CEOs	– Contextual effects	– **'Gestalt' effects'**		
Other top executives	– 'Regression to the mean'	– **Complexity, ambiguity and lack of experience**		
– role and process	– 'Less is more fallacy'	– Preference reversals		
– compensation	– **Mood-altered judgement**	– Mental accounting and choice bracketing		
– relations with Principals, employees, other parties	– **'Omission or commission bias'**	– **Satisficing**		
'External' nexus	– **Pattern-seeking**			
– Market for corporate control	– **Representativeness bias**			
– Corporate finance markets and intermediaries	– Availability bias			
– Gatekeepers	– Prospect Theory			
– Legal system and business law				
– Government policy				
– Other institutions (including informal ones)				
Economic system				
– business cycle effects				
– sectoral effects				

Note: **bolded items** indicate biases that are expected to be especially relevant in a corporate governance context with respect to Principals and Agents.

There are many possible ways to construct a table like this so the presentation is not meant to be definitive, just a starting point. The idea is as follows: a scale of different points in the internal and external nexus of firm governance is provided in the first column and the additional columns note the four major categories of behavioural characteristics of actors generally. Principals and Agents remain the two major sides in the core of the internal/external nexus but contextual parties are also introduced, including government and gatekeepers and corporate financiers. Additionally, and following the macroeconomic literature, economic system context is noted, i.e. the environment present by way of the business cycle and the sector within which a firm operates. Other dimensions, such as specific culture or country could be introduced but have been left out as these are not the major emphasis of this book.

The template then suggests a basic task, which is to consider how each individual human actor might be affected by known biases and heuristics at different points in the governance system. In particular, behavioural economics highlights that individuals might act one away alone and another when in a group and also that the process through which an individual interacts can affect outcomes meaningfully, sometimes more than the actual substance of the issues at hand. So within a firm one has to consider how shareholders act individually but also ask how they might coordinate with one another to form larger groupings which might skew their cognitions and decisions. Such groupings might be formal, as when there are concentrated holdings, or perhaps informal, for example, as when significant though not major shareholders might see each other socially and perhaps influence one another. There might be cases where internal dynamics of large shareholders occur, such as within pension funds or other institutional investors. And the nature of the actual corporate processes available for shareholder voice and exit need to be understood, such as the timing, locales, and agenda setting for annual meetings, all possible occasions for significant behavioural effects to occur. Analogous questions arise for Board members, individually and as a group, and similarly for different layers of top management. Downward as well as upward relationships are noted in the table as well, and in some firms, such as financial intermediaries, 'low-level' employees such as traders, may need to have special attention paid to them. Compensation is highlighted as an especially significant specific issue.

Although there are many different behavioural idiosyncrasies, not all are likely to be equally relevant or likely in a corporate governance setting. Partly this flows out of the fundamental assumptions of the underlying behavioural and governance theoretical models. Remember that these biases are posited as general deviations from presumed baseline tendencies of rationality, self-interest, maximisation and atomism. In other words, the research thus far is couched in terms of the 'average' person, with occasional attention paid to specialists and experts.

However, the core Principals and Agents in a business enterprise are probably dissimilar in certain ways to everyday people. There is a selection bias for one thing, in which more competitive, hard-charging, hard-headed and perhaps more rationalistic individuals are more likely to be large shareholders, business founders, and top executives than would be found in the general population.

And the competitive pressures of the marketplace do affect people and how they have to behave, or believe they have to. Marketplace culture is very competitive and this will cause key participants in that culture to have different values and perceptions and beliefs, which is what has been found even in experimental game contexts in which players often change they way they play based on something as simple from changing the name of the game to something like 'the business game' from a more technical 'prisoner's dilemma' moniker. Indeed the mere fact that there is a dominant model of economic behaviour with specific descriptions of how the 'ideal' actor 'should' act can affect how people actually do behave through social norming and other processes, an example of behavioural economics in action.

So some *a priori* suggestions regarding relevance are made above through the use of bolded terms for those biases that are expected to be most in evidence in corporate governance at the level of core Principal, Agent and significant actor. Most of the rationality biases are bolded because they have been shown to be exhibited in the greatest variety of situations and by the greatest variety of people, including experts and sophisticates. The same is true for the atomism biases which, far fewer in number, nonetheless also have been seen to be fairly universal in a general way, though their manifestations do vary by context and culture. Proportionately the maximisation and self-interest biases are expected to be the least present mainly because corporate leadership at all levels seems to exhibit a set of norms and dynamics distinct from the broader culture within which they sit. But, it needs to be said again, that these are prior assumptions for purposes of discussion. They do need to be examined more on both an empirical and theoretical level.

It also must be said that this template and their implied priorities represents those of behavioural economics and not those of other perspectives or even of the narrow behavioural economics field as it might develop in the future. That's why so much attention is given to psychology generally and cognitive/rational aspects in particular. A sociologist, for example, would consider sociality paramount, and perhaps rightly so, maybe even especially so in the often insular cultures of boardrooms and counting houses. Thus their list would be perhaps quite different from that provided above. Some alternative or complementary dimensions are therefore considered in the next chapter.

Overall this inventory could be used as a preliminary checklist when considering specific corporate cases or market settings or reviewing existing governance protocols, procedures and processes. It also has a policy use, as a way of filtering through existing or proposed legislation. So, for example, a government might puts its governance laws through this filter to see if major specific behavioural contingencies have been considered in legislative design. Essentially this template condenses the findings of the existing literature in a useable way, subject to amendment as knowledge grows.

Possible behavioural solutions

So far the discussion has been about the problem. What of the potential solutions that take into account human quirks? In many ways there is much more definitive to be said here since there are indeed quite a few devices out there for addressing human limitations, some tested, some less so. The task is to apply these to the corporate governance setting. Table 5.5 threads together some possible solutions to the process of corporate governance. This list is not completely developed and presents only one or a few ideas in each category. As already noted, and to be discussed a bit more in Chapter 6, the empirics are still relatively light as to how effective behavioural solutions such as 'nudges' are, so one could consider this a roadmap to further research as well.

This is a suggestive list rather than definitive, comprehensive or tested. It is focused on the major parties to the Principal/Agent nexus and could be extended into other areas of firm operations such as customer service and relations. The idea is that the major areas of corporate governance can be broken down into component processes and parts, tied back to established cognitive and other biases and then linked to solutions that are known to have some 'debiasing' impact.

A few clarifications and expansions are in order. First, two of the solutions above have been speculatively noted as 'probably not applicable': the use of present bias and of decoys. The basis for this supposition, and it is just that at this point, is that major Principals and Agents are generally forward looking and strategic in orientation and hence less prone to present bias in major decisions and that decoys are generally most applicable in lower level decision settings by less sophisticated actors, such as consumers reading through service agreements. That is not to say that, as humans, major corporate players do not suffer from these biases that might need to be corrected in these particular ways. And certainly these devices might be useful for actors engaged in other company activities. But they do seem to be likely inapplicable based on priors.

Second, this list of possible solutions are modifications to an existing conception and not at all a fundamental challenge to the governance paradigm in place. In that way it follows behavioural economics more generally which is not a challenge to the neoclassical way of thinking but simply an amendment to it, hopefully empirically informed. There is a real place for such an approach, not least because incremental changes can have real impact and yet can be added and experimented with in a relatively low cost way. But if the cycles of corporate failure and scandal have more fundamental causes that our current models miss and we reasonably hope to ameliorate these cycles then more thorough going measures may be necessary to lead to appreciable improvement in that regard.

Third, these devices can as easily be used to manipulate and deceive as they can be used to debias and clarify. Indeed, this is a major implicit problem with the entire 'nudges' approach by which this list and the research agenda underlying it is inspired. Many of these ideas have been well known to marketers and others who have used them, sometimes nefariously or at least with only narrow self-interest in mind, and in the 'wrong hands' they can and do mislead. Corporate

Table 5.5 Potential 'fixes' to behavioural deviations in corporate governance

General solution	Principal/Agent setting examples	Specific potential fixes
Change default options	– Board processes – Shareholder meetings	– 'Automatic' proxies (similar to automatic tax returns) – Changes to board voting protocols and agendas
Use present bias	[Probably not applicable]	[Probably not applicable]
Limit and simplify options	– Board processes – Shareholder consultations	– Simplification of board and shareholder meeting agendas
Strategically pick the form of incentives	– Executive compensation	– Strategic mix of non-monetary and monetary compensation to promote alignment of intrinsic and extrinsic motivation
Encourage looking at things differently	– Board meetings and processes – Design of engagements with other nexus actors, e.g. financiers	– Use of 'pre-mortems' before major internal and external firm decisions
Use social forces	– Board meetings and processes – Shareholder engagements and dynamics	– Change attendance protocols to key meetings to exclude parties likely to misalign Principals and Agents and include those likely to align them (e.g. not allowing attendance by CEO or COO at Board compensation or audit committee meetings)
Reframe things	– Board, shareholders and other key governance meetings at all levels	– Reframe agendas and choice sets to limit psychological biases
Structure decision support	– Management throughout the firm – Compliance with and design of regulation	– Issue structured compliance guides with new regulations for major Agents – Offer tested decision support for major risk management decisions
Utilise salience	– Corporate reporting	– Provide important and relevant details in reports to Boards, gatekeepers, shareholders, etc., in vivid form
Imagine alternatives	– Board processes	– Require Board to imagine alternatives in the event of contestable or contested decisions
Re-train	– Staff and executive development	– Require training in mission critical behavioural skills (e.g. formal statistics)

Re-design disclosure	– Customer and supplier relationships – Shareholder and investor relations	– Provide behaviourally informed annual reports
Provide cooling off periods	– Major strategic firm decisions	– Require major investment committee to have a cooling-off period for large projects over a certain threshold
Consider the opposite	– Board processes – Management decision-making	– Incorporate 'consider the opposite' protocols into key governance processes
Use decoys	[Probably not applicable]	[Probably not applicable]
Employ pre-commitment devices	– Employment contracts	– Pre-commit top executives in ways that align Principal and Agents
Practice, practice, practice	– Management and executive development and recruitment	– Develop, offer and/or require key decision-makers to take 'continuing education' in core behavioural skills such as statistical inference
Provide immediate feedback	– Shareholder relations – Oversight of management by owners	– Provide feedback throughout the year to top managers rather than just end of the year or quarterly (and distinct from compensation based 'performance reviews')
Understand differences in people	– Board member selection	– Evaluate Board members for thinking styles etc. and aim for diversity to avoid 'groupthink' and other biases
Use routines and algorithms in some instances	– Line operations of certain types	– Evaluate employees and suppliers based on validated and simple schemata

Agents might find ways to abuse these devices to further Principal–Agent misalignment and become more efficient at it to boot. Thus, for example, 'automatic proxies' which might be established with 'benign' defaults to ensure full and reasoned participation in shareholder votes can obviously be misused to allow management to take full control of a company. It is not obvious how this problem can be avoided in practice and it must be seriously considered in any proposal for change.

Which raises a fourth point which is about values. Like all philosophies, neoclassical economics has a set of implicit values and behavioural economics imports these in, the two major ones being consequentalism (or utilitarianism more specifically) and libertarianism (or consumer sovereignty more narrowly). The former value holds that actions can and should be judged by their consequences primarily and not by any intrinsic standard, while the latter holds that individuals should be compelled by external authority as little as possible.

Without getting into debating the merits of these values, it is important to realise that they exist within the theory, if hidden. And there are important questions that are unresolved in such ideals, especially the use and abuse of power, private or public. For example, it is not always clear that unconstrained individual choice is always a good thing, even for the individual concerned. The abuse of government power is obviously a real threat, often observed in practice. But at the extreme, libertarianism holds that most private actions should be allowed, including sale of one's organs for profit, discrimination against individual groups in the provision of strictly privately provided services, and no regulation of 'underage' drinking and drug use. How does one guarantee that corporate or other private power will not be abused and how can one be sure that the weak parties in a transaction are actually 'consenting' to their choice? Additionally how should one judge use of power, appropriate or otherwise, without some sort of agreed upon moral or ethical benchmark? Other than assuming that the 'market' will cure all, which even in purely neoclassical terms cannot be guaranteed, corporate nudges, even if well-intentioned or even effective in behavioural terms, might not lead to 'moral' or 'ethical' outcomes. Consequentalism is very weak standard in this regard, even when it works, for there are many possible Pareto-optimal scenarios, some of which might offend general society. These problems are not easy to resolve, but they must be noted and they are mostly ignored in the current behavioural discourse.

Fifth, a few of the ideas mentioned above have actually made it into public policy and a few more have been mooted in the academic literature. Board process and institutional investor behaviour in particular has been addressed in UK corporate governance law especially and in US regulation to a lesser degree, including prescriptions about CEO attendance at Board meetings, the independence and competence of directors, and the transparency of nominating processes amongst other things. Not all of these were or are behaviourally informed but some are, especially after the Global Financial Crisis when the field of behavioural economics and finance had already infused much of the broad dialogue and drew new attention and energy. The UK and Irish Auditing Practices Board (APB) of the UK Financial Reporting Council (Financial Reporting Council 2012) also has issued a paper on professional scepticism as a useful stance to take in auditing activities since it makes individuals question their possibly biased priors.

On the academic side, the literature review on boards by Van Ees et al. (2009) notes that studies have looked at governance behavioural issues including: small group decision making; the influence of director competency, experience, and knowledge on effective board functioning and strategic decisions; Board appointments and social network ties; existing norms of appropriate beliefs and behaviours in a relevant industry or country; processes of social construction and symbolism; imitation with Boards and management; and socialisation processes and rhetoric and impression management and custom. And this is just in the mainly economics-oriented inquiries (that include other disciplinary lines of inquiry such as strategic management). Sociological, anthropological, psychological and ethnographic approaches, to name just a few, would reveal other dimensions. The main preferred contribution of the list above is that draws existing ideas for governance process reform together in a concrete way specifically mapped into governance structures and actors, not that the individual issues have not been studied, though there is also much to be done.

Sixth, and finally, there is an implicit behavioural paradox underlying all this which is also present in the literature itself. For if you seek to outwit a clever human with 'tricks' what is to stop them from learning and outwitting you back? This is not a critique per se but simply a recognition that human psychology is changeable and malleable and that as the behavioural literature becomes incorporated into mainstream knowledge actors will adapt and policy prescriptions that might work at one time might no longer work at a later time as people get wise to what is going on.

Or not. For if these really are persistent and at least quasi-universal fundamentals of human mental models they will not change easily or at all. Even this basic question does not yet have a definitive answer. While some of the existing writing suggests the discovery of immutable laws of human action and decision the fundamental science is far from settled or established.

A summing up

What to take away from this discussion? One conclusion is that there is a core set of findings from behavioural economics that has potential utility in correcting for some known malfunctions that are based in known limitations of human psychology. Another is that these findings can be and need to be applied in specific ways to specific elements of overall governance structure, which is what this chapter has attempted to do in a basic and preliminary way.

It is also true that much more needs to be done to refine and test both the suggestions laid out here and to develop new ones. And the overall effectiveness of these devices from a systemic point of view remains to be seen. It may be that more structural rethinking is needed both theoretically and practically or at least that the intellectual ecosystem of the mainstream needs to be expanded. To this topic the next and final chapter turns.

6 The future understanding of corporate governance

So now we arrive at the end of the book. Up to now the ground covered has been fairly narrow: Neoclassical Economic Theory and its offspring of neoclassical Corporate Governance Theory; the findings of behavioural economics and a catalogue of some of its suggestions for correcting for human 'biases' generally; a review of themes of corporate governance misfires of the past and the standard diagnoses and prescriptions these have engendered; and a preliminary application of the findings and suggestions of behavioural economics to corporate governance and the building of an initial investigatory framework.

Now there will be a look up from the analytical ground to the blue skies above. For the argument that has been made here consistently is that while behavioural economics is a move in a good direction and that there is utility in applying its findings to corporate governance, nonetheless the research and policy project this represents is incremental at best for a situation that calls out for more departures from accepted mental models that may no longer be an acceptable summary of reality. This chapter therefore attempts to present and discuss some of the fundamental questions about future directions that have thus far been mostly hinted at and makes some suggestions about where to go from here.

To preview the end of the journey this examination will point to the need to identify those domains best suited for particular theoretical approaches with the ultimate ideal (in this author's mind) of an ecosystem of models of corporate governance that co-exist and interact with one another to yield a more robust set of concepts, theories and policies. The neoclassical paradigm, even a behaviourally informed one, should not continue its primacy of place in this author's view; and, granted, this is an argument surely to be rejected by many economists other than myself. But conversely neither should economics be relegated to a trash heap of history as some might hope, for it has real power and utility in appropriate but limited domains, the same which could be said for most other theories as well.

'It takes a theory to beat a theory'

First, a substantial amount of time needs to be spent on a methodological issue that has proven to be a block to more integrative discourse. This is the supposed parsimony and power of the neoclassical model itself. Granted, if that model is as predictively powerful and economical as its adherents say it is, then its centrality is a good thing, made even better by some empirically supported details that make it richer and more useful in psychological detail, such as those of behavioural economics.

This presumption, however, is a shibboleth that needs revision and probably demolition. Despite a huge literature on economic methodology written over the decades by economists and others that should have torn down 'economic imperialism' (to use Lazear's phrase (2000)) a long time ago, or more correctly, put it into proper perspective, the paradigm lives on with more vehement support from some quarters than ever. Arguably neoclassical economics has become an ideology in many ways more than a theory in some of its practice, and ideology is never a friend to truth in the end even if it points out some true things.

A definitive right-sizing of neoclassicism (my true aim, not an attack) cannot be accomplished or even attempted here. If economists such as Boulding (1969), Frey (2001), Sen (1970/1984; 1977) and many others could not do this, certainly this author cannot. But the basic issues about methodological fitness need to be reviewed before building up to a theoretical holism, which many economists still reject and find abhorrent (Lazear 2000; Becker 1976).

The debate over the fitness of one theory over another is often captured by the saying that 'it takes a theory to beat a theory', the literal meaning of which is unclear, but which economic and Coasean legal theorists use to say that that the neoclassical core cannot be challenged until its opponents come up with a structure which is superior to it. The phrase, used by neoclassical law and economics scholar Richard Posner in a 1983 article, is often attributed to Gary Becker (Epstein 1983).

What makes for a superior theory? By no means is that a settled question generally but the basic criteria proposed by economists boil down to two in this context: parsimony and predictive power. A third criterion is the suitability and realism of assumptions but, oddly, economic methodologists hold this to be a less important issue, about which more will be said below.

Parsimony is a theoretical ideal that follows the medieval epigram of 'Ockham's Razor' (sometimes spelled 'Occam's Razor') which, translated from the Latin reads, 'Entities should not be multiplied unnecessarily.' This means that simpler theories with identical predictions are to be preferred to more complicated theories (hence the proscription on unnecessary 'entities' or theoretical components) (Gibbs (Hiroshi) 1996/1997).

That last part about 'identical predictions' is almost universally lost in the debate about the neoclassical versus other models of human behaviour. It is claimed that neoclassical economics is more parsimonious than other theories such as those of psychologists and while that may be true (or not, as shall be argued later) in fact conceptual apples are usually being compared to oranges. For almost always, theories grounded in other disciplines do not predict exactly the same things as those of certain brands of economics.

Even within the economics discipline there are theoretical variants that do not agree with one another predictively and whose relative parsimony is thus not easy to compare. Macroeconomic versus microeconomic constructions of the business cycle are a good example: classical theories are simpler than Keynes' conception, but the former predicts that business cycles will always re-equilibrate while the latter predicts that this is not necessarily the case. This is why Keynes adds assumptions, to explain why this might occur, arguing that the predictions of his theory are closer to reality than those of the neoclassicists of his time (and why he called their theory a 'special case' of the 'General Theory' he was trying to create).

In physics and other hard sciences Ockham's Razor is easier to apply in practice since the characteristics of the phenomena being studied are often beyond dispute, at least during a given period of observation. Thus the theory that there was an 'ether' through which light travelled and which explained some of its seemingly odd observed properties was overthrown by a combination of new and more accurate empirical observation and Einstein's Theory of Relativity which not only did away with the assumption of an ether but also the Newtonian assumption of an independent time and space, thus getting both better congruence with empirics and a simplification of underlying assumptions (Gibbs (Hiroshi) 1996/1997).

In inquiries into humanity the task is not nearly as clear-cut. For example, a sociologist has this to say about neoclassical 'parsimony': '[It] is a problem, not a solution, if for the sake of simplicity it disregards the moral, i.e. social foundation of human action; if it abstracts from the historical context of human life and from the non-quantifiable content of the shared meanings that define it' (Streeck 2010: 396). 'Charles Darwin referred to man as a "moral being" and that underlies human capacity for "agency", for stepping back and deliberating about what course of action is right or wrong' (Streeck 2010: 395). Of course one can argue about whether the moral impulse of human beings should be added to a theory of behaviour but already the premises and predictions of the sociological versus the economic theory are quite different from the start. That one is supposedly more 'complex' than another does not attest to their relative merits from a pure theory standpoint. One has to consider what the predictions of each model really are to then be able to sift through them on the basis of 'parsimony'.

One has to ask how parsimonious the Economic Theory really is anyway. In fact people might do well to go back to some of the original writings on cognitive theory where Simon himself critiques the neoclassical behavioural model as relying on a slew of implicit yet auxiliary assumptions that he says its predictions actually rely upon (Simon 1957, 1962).

Instructive of neoclassical views of their own assumptions is this quote from the Camerer and Loewenstein (2004), deans of the current behavioural economics field if any are:

> As Arrow (1986) pointed out, economic models do not derive much predictive power from the single tool of utility-maximization. Precision comes from the drill bits – such as time-additive separable utility in asset pricing, including a child's utility into a parent's utility function to explain bequests, rationality

of expectations for some applications and adaptive expectations for others, homothetic preferences for commodity bundles, price-taking in some markets and game-theoretic reasoning in others, and so forth (2004: 42).

Besides the assumption of the existence of a utility function itself, which seems to have passed into the realm of fact here, the use of the 'drill bits' is highly misleading for these are not mere appendages but are actually additional and, one could argue, strong and specific assumptions, and thus hardly parsimonious. The debate over whether neoclassicism is parsimonious or not remains a fraught issue in the academic discourse but it is one in which some economists' claims for it should not be taken for granted.

But what about that claim that neoclassical models make better predictions than other models? Neoclassical economists argue that their model is superior on this count especially. This, however, is far from as cut and dried as many economists seem to think. There are two problems: (1) what is the economic model actually predicting; and (2) what constitutes solid empirical validation of those predictions? These are nettlesome issues even for highly empirical fields but they are especially difficult for the social sciences. Although to hear some economists talk it seems not so for economics.

In a broad sense the neoclassical model seems to have very clear predictions such as maximisation and self-interest. But we have already seen how while these seem intuitively clear and simple, conceptually they are not easy to pin down and practically can cover a wide range of observed behaviours. So a society might be seen to have actors who stiff everyone but themselves, including family members, up through to others who live simply and give generously to friends, family and charity. This diversity can be said to conform to the predictions of the model that people will always maximise their utility and are self-interested in doing so.

Why? Because utility is a very malleable concept. Perhaps the stingy person's utility function is being maximised just as much as the generous person's simply because their utility functions are different. Now both outcomes can be justified as 'consistent' with the model's predictions, especially if one chooses a few choice 'drill bits' to tweak problem areas. Obviously this is a less than satisfactory situation for the theory always seems to win, which can suggest the presence of tautology. Many practitioners in many different disciplines are certainly guilty of this too, but economics in general cannot unquestionably be said to be better than those other fields, just, perhaps, more confident.

In many ways this is why there exists a debate at all about whether behavioural economics is consistent with, or a departure from, the neoclassical model. If that model had very tightly defined predictions it would not be possible to sustain this debate for any period of time. Either the speed of light is constant or it is not. But maybe human biases and heuristics actually are consistent with maximisation and rationality, as some argue. It depends upon how you look at it and what time frame – short run or long run – that you use. Is it consistent or isn't it? This is not yet clear from the literature and it is a very basic question. This is a serious methodological problem that should inspire humility rather than the often aggressive stance taken by some economists and their sympathisers. The more fruitful approach to resolving it would be gather more evidence rather than retreat to first principles.

This is not to say that the neoclassical model has no validity or applicability in the real world. To take but one example, land prices in most areas follow a 'rent gradient' i.e. a fall in unit prices as one moves further out from the centre of a city. This accords with the predictions of urban economics which says that central locations are more 'efficient' when transport costs are taken into account, being closer to customers and suppliers, hence cheaper to service markets from, and hence more expensive to locate in (actors have to pay a premium to account for their economisation of transport costs).

This example is an application of the more general neoclassical model which is highly simplified and much more crude than the variety of real world locations it attempts to describe. Yet it is a very specific tailoring of that model to a limited and definite set of phenomenon with outcomes that can be relatively objectively measured and which can be seen to predict and explain quite well in a wide variety of settings. This sort of thing is what some behavioural economists are arguing for, namely an application of the more general neoclassical model to a well-defined domain which, as yet, however, is still in the process of being clearly defined.

But this is not what many other writers are aiming for, which is either to keep behavioural observations out of economics altogether, or appending it to the existing core without correspondent limitation to areas where it works best. This has added a lot of heat but not much light to an important area of inquiry and the debate surrounding it.

Human behaviour and the internal processes associated with them are notoriously difficult to fathom in any case. There are many validated observations but as of yet no truly accepted general theory. This is why psychology has so many competing schools of thought and so many small bore specialities. Behavioural economics does offer a tantalising possibility of a relatively neat paradigm that has potentially fruitful applications in some areas. But the greater attention should be focused on finding and testing those applications in various areas to see what works best where instead of warring over which theory is better than another.

As for validation more generally, Loewenstein (1999: F26) distinguishes between internal validity (i.e. the ability to draw confident causal conclusions from one's research) and external validity (i.e. the ability to generalise from the research context to the settings that the research is intended to approximate). He notes that one sometimes has to trade off one for the other. For example, Experimental Economics, which uses contrived experiments in an artificial setting, has the advantage of high internal validity but there are real questions when it comes to its external validity. The psychological literature has a similar divide between highly experimental studies and much more applied and contextual clinical work and could be said to grapple with the two types of validity as well.

There are real ambiguities around empirical validation of psychological phenomena. Rubinstein (2007: 1244) notes that most brain studies attempt to make inferences based on brain neural activity but also says that there are many more obvious physical indicators of the way in which people reason, such as mouse clicks and eye movements, that are easier to capture and perhaps easier to interpret.

Neural scans however seem to be preferred by many neoclassically oriented writers, probably because they appear to be precise and fit well into preconceived notions of theoretical parsimony as well as the formalisation which neoclassical exposition favours.

Camerer's 2007 article on neuroeconomics is worth extracting from to show this. '[T]heories that can explain neural facts and choices should have some advantage over theories which explain only choices, if they are comparably tractable' (2007: C39). 'The importance of circuitry also implies that the right kinds of models are computational ones in which well-understood components collaborate to create behaviour' (C29) '... being in equilibrium is not merely a mathematical restriction on equality of choices and beliefs, it is also a "state of mind" identifiable in brain imaging' (C35).

> The idea that a firm just combines labour and capital is obviously a gross simplification...The *new* theory of the *firm* replaces the (perennially useful) fiction of a *profit-maximising firm* which has a single goal, with a more detailed account of how *components* of the *firm* – *individuals, hierarchies* and *networks* – interact and communicate to determine *firm* behaviour. Neuroeconomics proposes to do the same by treating an individual economic Agent like a firm ... The *neuroeconomic* theory of the *individual* replaces the (perennially useful) fiction of a *utility-maximising individual* which has a single goal, with a more detailed account of how *components* of the *individual* – *brain regions, cognitive control*, and *neural circuits* – interact and communicate to determine *individual* behaviour (Camerer 2007: C37; emphasis in original).

Note how reductionist this is and how easily implicit assumptions slip in, especially the analogy of circuits which tends to drive the conclusions about neural activity. The description of the theory of the firm and the comparison made with the theory of the human being is rather breath-taking in its audacity, and equally so in its debatability, despite being presented as obvious. And the notion that all neural circuits 'calculate' is questionable in and of itself as the interpretation of brain imaging is not straightforward. As quoted above, neural analysis is not as simple or definite as Camerer makes it seem.

A strong and somewhat ad hominem response to this specific neural focus is offered by Piore (2010):

> The problem with behavioural economics, as I see it, is basically that it is committed to rooting economic behaviour in individual psychology and ultimately tracing that psychology to the biological construction of the human brain. It thus leads directly to what is rapidly becoming a distinct branch, neuro-economics. In the extreme, this leads to a willingness to

improve economic outcomes through biological intervention. It need not, of course, be carried to this extreme. But it does pick up a strand of thought in American economics in particular which led the discipline in the late nineteenth and early twentieth centuries to become closely associated with Social Darwinism (2010: 385).

Of course a critique not need go this far, nor probably should it, but the mechanistic orientation of neuroeconomics especially is something that should be interrogated more than it has been.

The neoclassical/behavioural approach is also rigidly deductive, relying on specification of assumptions and inferences first, and then seeking empirical validation later. Thus it eschews any hint of the alternative approach of induction in which generalities are built up from the particulars of empirical observation. One approach is not better than the other, just more or less useful depending upon the problem. And induction and deduction interact with one another in actual scientific discovery anyway, and not always distinctly but messily, very humanly indeed. This is why induction is often relegated to the 'inferior' position of policy when economists write about it. To take one of many indicative quotes: '[B]ehavioural economics is proving (and is likely to continue to be) more important for prescriptions than explanation' (Heap 2013: 993).

Of course one obvious thing seems to have been neglected thus far and that is the realism or plausibility of the assumptions of a theory. One would think this to be critical. Yet economic methodology has an eccentric position in this regard, influenced as it is by a famous article by the economist Milton Friedman in which he argued that the only thing that matters in judging an economic theory is its ability to make empirically validated predictions (Friedman 1953).

We've already seen the difficulties of validation but this Friedmanite construct is something separate from that (and the actual mechanics of validation is not a process Friedman considers much anyway). Camerer (2007: C26) outlines Friedman's argument as follows. Given A (assumptions) and P (predictions) of a theory two arguments follow. (1) False A should be tolerated if they give good P. (2) A should be judged by accuracy of P, as mathematically implied.

Camerer notes that this so-called 'F-twist' has had numerous implications, not least of which was is its relegation of realistic actor psychology to the sidelines of economics. 'Economic theories that assume that individual agents are highly rational and willful, judge probabilities accurately, and maximise their own wealth might prove useful, even though psychology shows that those assumptions are systematically false. The F twist allowed economists to ignore psychology' (Camerer 1999: 10575).

Indeed one can see economists' continuing acceptance of Friedman's stance on assumptions by the fact that no matter how much psychologists, sociologists and others assail the neoclassical approach with evidence of how absurd its blanket premises seem to be, economists point to its supposed predictive power and parsimony as proof of its superiority and the rightness of ignoring seemingly contrary evidence. Except the truth of these assumptions is now so strongly believed in that gone is the idea that these are simply useful fictions with predictive power.

Camerer notes an additional problem with this sort of thinking (and he is not the only one to do so). Camerer refers to the 'hidden repair condition'. To continue to use his notation, P is probably driven by some hidden A that should be uncovered rather than just relying on the false A. 'A' more grounded in 'psychological and neuroscientific facts' would make a theory with good 'P' stronger and perhaps eliminate or identify any hidden assumptions (Camerer 2007: C27). This parallels the critique of neoclassical theory made by Simon and others that it relies on hidden auxiliary assumptions that need to be tested to support its strong predictions.

This may seem like a long excursion into pure methodology but attention needs to be paid because right now this is the major fault line between economics and other disciplines, at least in the mainstream discourse about behavioural economics. If one hopes to build a more cooperative interdisciplinary research agenda into cause and effect in corporate governance, this methodological divide needs to be understood if it is to be bridged. And even Einstein admitted that while the elegance of human constructs was a desirable discipline to adhere to in developing theory, the universe itself might in fact behave in a more complicated way than humans believed. If one discovers this, it is the simple theory that must go, not the more complex reality.

Some new frontiers

Assuming that methodological tolerance – but not sloppiness – can ultimately prevail, what are some of the next frontiers in a behavioural inquiry into corporate governance? The rest of this chapter will consider 10 critical issues to be dealt with as the field of behavioural approaches develops and expands. There certainly will be others, and those most pertinent to economics are emphasised below. But if academics, practitioners and policymakers give due consideration to these things it is argued that the outcome will be a more relevant and useful corporate governance field and hopefully a lessening of the cycle of actual governance boom and bust if principles arising are applied in practice.

The 10 critical issues are:

1   morality, ethics and values
2   sociality
3   Expanding the definition of Principal and corresponding agency
4   accounting for the rest of the body – its not just about the brain.
5   embodiment generally
6   determining relevant domains
7   useful empirics
8   behavioural finance
9   a macroeconomic–microeconomic synthesis
10 dynamic capabilities and key actor psychologies

Morality, ethics and values

One central feature of human society is the distinctly human realm of morality, ethics and values. It has already been noted the economics relies on a notion of morality both implicit and unexamined. Thaler and Sunstein (2009) thus prefer to rely on 'Nudging' which draws from the authors' preferred libertarianism, an attitude they share with most of the economic writing in the behavioural field and beyond.

This implicit moral approach and explicitly amoral framing is unacceptable as an organising principle for a number of reasons. First, in corporate governance the moral and ethical dimension is often the central one and many failures stem from a lack of attention to both, as can be seen during the Global Financial Crisis when an 'anything goes' ethos was certainly part of the problem and a definite hindrance to the solution. The neoclassical approach abstracts away from morality by assuming that the solution to governance is optimal contracting which seeks to limit efficiency-reducing rent-seeking activities by Agents and others. This is as close to morality and ethics that the theory gets but it is not close enough for all it refers to is rational maximisation, something the model contends everyone does and as fundamentally desirable in and of itself, or at least natural. However, corruption is a core facet of a lot of governance problems and that would seem to be more than just an exercise in improperly constrained individual rational maximisation. Corrupt behaviour can encompass simple rent-seeking but some of its variants have a moral and ethical dimension that is uniquely human and a psychological aspect that can veer into the wantonly self-destructive, something that does not accord well with neoclassical ideas set within mild behavioural bounds.

Second, policy especially has to have a set of values by which to assess public and private actions and design appropriate collective responses (and to determine when actors should not be interfered with and when collective response would thus be harmful). What these values are and should be will always be contested and contestable but the default should not be an unquestioned libertarianism whose efficacy is based on a consequentialism drawn from an assumption of a benevolent market sorting things out. Even on these terms consequences themselves need to be judged and a crude consumer sovereignty is not an obvious standard to use given the potentially wide variety of preferences consumers will have. And when activities are not clearly economic in nature, the consumer sovereignty standard can be even more problematic, the radical views of Gary Becker and other neoclassicists who reduce all activity to economic activity notwithstanding.

Finally, the moral impulse is a core characteristic of human psychology and being generally. Classical economics in fact sprung out of moral philosophy and Adam Smith had a keen interest in morality as evidenced by the many observations about human morality that pepper *The Wealth of Nations* and his other major work *The Theory of Moral Sentiments*. John Stuart Mill, another giant of the classical era in economics, was a major writer on moral and ethical philosophy and indeed may be credited with (or blamed for) the introduction of libertarianism and utilitarianism into the discipline of economics. Indeed it was not until the end of the nineteenth century that moral discourse was subsumed and covered over by the formal models of Jevons and Marshall, a process that continues today (Barber 2010). Indeed some of the examples of 'bias', such as a concern with fairness or 'failure' to maximise might be motivated more by moral impulse than anything else and hence should be a legitimate locus of study and not just a sideline for professional ethicists. Sociologists on this very point have already been quoted earlier.

One interesting example of an approach to morality applied to corporate governance which builds off the Agency model as a framework is offered by Morck (2008). He distinguishes between a 'Type I Agency problem', in which an individual acts for herself when social welfare would be higher if she acted instead as a proper Agent while a 'Type II Agency Problem' exists when an individual acts as an Agent when social welfare would be higher if she acted for herself (or more properly speaking her conscience).

Morck claims that traditional governance theorists, such as Jensen and Meckling, are concerned with Type I problems, while Milgrom, whose research Morck adapts to the governance context, is more concerned with Type 2 problems. 'Soldiers who pilfer from army stores constitute a type I agency problem; soldiers who fire on civilians when ordered to constitute a type II agency problem' (2008: 194). One possible solution to Type II problems is to create a formal and powerful official with a duty to criticise, a sort of rival (moral) authority figure to the established power structure (2008: 194). Examples are the academic discussant/ referee model and official Leaders of the Opposition (perhaps now applied to the boardroom) (2008: 195–196). This sort of thinking could be said to be implicitly behind the enhanced whistleblower protections added in the SOX act in the US, though in fact these have been little used, partly because of poor implementation and partly, and perhaps more importantly, because of threats of retaliation by superiors if whistleblowing was discovered (Lipman 2012). Some interesting thinking on morality and ethics in a corporate governance setting is out there and more needs to be developed.

Sociality

Morality and ethics arguably spring from the all important characteristic of human sociality. This has not been ignored by economists by any means, as has already been seen in the macroeconomic sphere and by prominent microeconomists such as Bruce McFadden (McFadden 2010).

In fact the social nature of human beings, rather than their rationality or psychology, may need to be a major focus by interdisciplinary scholars and not just left to sociologists who have done this for a long time and have been vehement advocates for bringing this dimension into the behavioural economics field. Without being as single-minded, this author agrees.

The field of economic sociology is a good bridge across which economists and sociologists especially should cross over and meet one another. One definition of economic sociology is: '[T]he application of the frames of reference, variables, and explanatory models of sociology to that complex of activities concerned with the production, distribution, exchange and consumption of scarce goods and services.' Smelser, who proposed this definition in 1963 referred to things such as personal interaction, groups, social structures (institutions) and social controls such as norms, values and sanctions has since been expanded by others to include 'every mode of production is a transaction with nature' and 'what a society is *prepared* to extract from nature' (Smelser and Swedberg 2010: 3).

The ways in which sociologists differ from economists in this area is instructive, e.g. seeing the economic actor as influenced and part of other groups versus being uninfluenced by them (so-called 'methodological individualism' in the former case); rationality seen as a variable versus rationality as an assumption; constraints on economic action being determined not by scarcity alone and its interaction with exogenous tastes but also by social structure and its meaning; society as always the basic reference point against which the market is compared rather than the other way around; a consideration of power relations instead of the microeconomic regard of actors as solely equals in exchange; the role of social institutions in noneconomic choices especially (e.g. while economists would regard crime as a rational individual choice, sociologists would see that as driven in part by and inseparable from social relations such as neighbourhood peer groups, etc.) (Smelser and Swedborg 2010: 3–6).

As Durkheim (1888) said: '[T]he man that economists talk about, this systematic egoist, is little but an artificial man of reason. The man that we know, the real man, is so much more complex: he belongs to a time and a country, he lives somewhere, he has a family, a country, a religious faith and political ideas' (Smelser and Swedborg 2010: 11). It is time that Corporate Governance Theory fully accounts for this reality.

Expanding the definition of Principal and corresponding agency

A long-established theory of corporate governance is Stakeholder Theory which holds that the shareholder is not the only or sometimes even the primary Principal to a firm. We have already seen how even mainstream corporate governance thinking sees the firm as a nexus and how research has expanded the view of which actors are relevant subjects of study in that nexus. The stakeholder model is one theory that can feed into this thinking.

There is also the more recent field of stewardship theory which has psychological and sociological influences explicitly built into it. Broadly speaking, this theory holds that, even in the case of Principal/Agent interest misalignments, the Agent might still act in accordance with the Principal's interests if doing so might result in opportunities for desired nonpecuniary personal outcomes such as achievement and status affiliation (Davis et al. 1997; Tosi et al. 2003). More fundamentally, it is often the case that both Principal and Agents often end up taking up shared stewardship of an entity through mutual identification with it, in which case any misalignment disappears (Sundaramurthy and Lewis 2003).

These two schools of thought are counterpoints to the reign of 'methodological individualism' that has been seen as a useful simplification but which is now facing a growing recognition that besides being blatantly unrealistic in many regards, alternative concepts of actor boundaries can in fact be more concordant with facts on the ground and hence valuable extensions or additions to some applications of theory. Indeed the notion of corporate culture is a recognition that people often identify with things much larger than themselves and perhaps act in ways sometimes contrary to their own self-interest narrowly defined, or perhaps in service to a self bigger than just an individual.

Neoclassically based behavioural economics already has introduced known deviations from self-interested behaviour. But this remains firmly rooted in atomistic individuals in competition with one another as a theoretical base so far. There are clearly times when this model accords with reality well. But other times it does not. Any new and expanded corporate governance approach should identify and study the arenas in which the individual actor is equal to, less than or more than themselves in isolation and how such re-identification might change their agency and their resulting decisions.

Accounting for the rest of the body – it's not just about the brain

Kahneman's description of his collaboration with Tversky and how they arrived at their "ah ha" moments of insight is both familiar and interesting as he emphasises particularly the role of their long walks together and being out in nature as important for fostering a non-critical attitude towards each other and being conducive to their best work (Kahneman 2011). Creativity and inspiration are well known to be associated with periods where the mind is not active and often inspired by physical activity that is not mental.

The very name 'cognitive revolution' to refer to the shift in psychological thinking that underlies behavioural economics shows an obsession with the head to the detriment of the rest of the body. Yet much information is received and processed by parts of the body other than the brain and human action is also animal action and driven by distinctly non-mental things, at least in certain times and places.

Seemingly absent from the behavioural economics literature are studies or ideas about how non-brain based characteristics of the human body affect perception, cognition, choice and action. These things are very present in the marketing and design literature, if not necessarily always modelled causally; there, correlations between characteristics and outcomes, such as increased purchases, are the main concern and replicability rather than explanation is usually considered enough to know.

But such considerations can be expanded upon in the service of shared understanding. Future study of corporate governance should consider much more the physicality of all parties to the corporate nexus. So, for example, rather than just studying Board member social connections, one might also consider member lifestyles, their level of physical activity, and the look and feel of the rooms they meet in as potential and significant potential affecters of decisions.

Embodiment generally

The behavioural literature already recognises the importance of context which basically says that form matters in some instances. The endowment effect is a clear example in which $10 in the form of sports cap, say, is treated differently by Agents depending upon whether they own the cap or not. The embodied tangibility of the cap extends to the tangibility of ownership and that makes a difference to people. It is quite probable that this is not just a matter of cognitive bias, the basic stance of the literature at present, but a deeper issue of the way in which the human physical form interacts with other physical forms.

This is a point that almost seems too obvious to make and many laypeople would say something like 'duh', to put it colloquially. From a research point of view it is nonetheless important to measure what the effects might or might not be, how large they are and how they change with circumstances.

Which is already being done to a degree though more care may need to make sure these things are captured properly when being researched. Here is an example. Kahneman's book is fairly (though not 100% exclusively) cognitive in its terms especially with heuristic analogies such as 'substitution' where he says people exchange easier questions (e.g. 'How do dolphins make me feel?') for harder ones (e.g. 'Should we protect species?'). A problem with putting things this way, besides being entirely head- and cognition-based, is that it implicitly assumes the comparability of such questions. Which may not be how humans actually process things and which may be misleading when built into experimental design in which people are offered such a choice as if it were equivalent (Kahneman 2011).

Embodiment is very important in many human activities, though this word is not often used. The way in which people learn is a prime example. In his book Kahneman notes his differences with Gary Klein and the Naturalist Decision Making (NDM) school of thought. The two differ on the role of intuition in learning. They actually collaborated to came to a sort of agreement that in environments where there is sufficient predictability and ability to learn regularities through prolonged practice, intuition, which Kahneman follows Simon in seeing it as a process of recognition (re-cognition), can actually lead to good decisions by experts rather than errors like the curse of knowledge. Examples of settings where this would be the case are chess moves and fire-fighting. In situations where this does not apply, heuristics and biases can be expected to dominate and thus expert 'intuition' needs to be corrected for. Examples: stock picking and political predictions. Kahneman provides many examples of other fields, one being anaesthesiology, where experts can observe immediate effects of their work and so their intuition is good while radiologists do not and so theirs is not so good. This can apply within a trade, e.g. a psychotherapist is good at knowing how to get a reaction out of a patient but not so much how a particular therapy will work long term (Kahneman 2011: 235–242).

The term embodiment is not used in this discussion but it does apply for what Kahneman is talking about is the form experience actually takes. It does make a difference in systematic ways. Corporate governance research could fruitfully benefit from this template to break different governance tasks and processes down into their specific manifestations to see whether persistent behavioural problems arise and how they might be addressed.

Determining relevant domains

This point has already been made but let's reiterate it: different disciplines and approaches should aim to be complementary to each other when possible (recognising that there will always be legitimate conflicts and disagreements about what constitutes truth). Thus neoclassical insight might be excellent in domains where its basic working assumptions hold best, e.g. highly competitive environments between culturally competitive strangers, but not so well in others, e.g. interactions within a close-knit group of shareholders from a highly social culture. Which is not to say that disciplinary turf should be laid out. Everything should always be open to question and investigation. But it is good to know generally that some areas are more penetrable by sonar, while others are better investigated with a searchlight, and not demand that one single approach be dominant.

Useful empirics

Huse (2005) notes that fewer than one out of eight of the empirical company board articles published in the leading scientific management journal was about actual board behaviour at the time his literature review was produced. Van Ees et al. (2009) have taken a stab at a potential framework for behaviourally based governance research and have noted both the relative paucity of empirical research on actual behaviour of boards and other parties to the corporate nexus and, more remarkably, note that where behavioral research on boards has been conducted, it has remained within the dominant agency paradigm for the most part. The empirics on actual corporate governance behaviour is scattered piecemeal, and often highly specialised.

The economistic bias towards deduction and away from induction, a view that has contaminated much of the business and social sciences, has probably contributed to this state of affairs. Robust theorising is still needed but so is systematic and preferably somewhat coordinated testing of propositions in the real world. And there should be nothing wrong with parallel tracks of deductive theory validation and building theory from the ground up based on good, solid and simple empirical observation.

Behavioural finance

This book has focused on behavioural economics but a perhaps even bigger field is behavioural finance. The basics are the same, i.e. a study of how actors deviate from the standard neoclassical assumptions and how this affects financial behaviour and markets. In many ways finance is a realm where neoclassical presumptions should hold most validity with generally liquid, deep and competitive markets with constant arbitrage activity and relatively anonymous and atomistic actors in many settings. Yet even here there have been found to be systematic deviations from 'Efficient Markets' with not only instances of irrational behaviour but irrational behaviour with sometimes severe consequence and with the same 'mistakes' being made over and over again (Barberis and Thaler 2003; Subrahmanyam 2008; Forbes 2009). Of course the financial sector has often been ground zero for wider economic consequence that propagates through the rest of the economy which has helped make for a popular reputation that most finance decisions are based on greed and fear (Avgouleas 2009).

Behavioural finance is very data intensive because many rich datasets are available and additionally real world repeatability of natural experiments is possible. Because of this behavioural finance has had more of an impact on finance generally (an applied economics field) than behavioural economics has had on economics more generally. Yet data satisfactory to orthodox economists has clearly shown standard economic assumptions to be in need of revision. There does need to be more cross-fertilisation between the empirics of the finance field with that of economics.

One particularly institutionally oriented version of behavioural finance is offered by Haugen (2003) who discusses the way in which, amongst other things, risk and reward are actually often positively rather than negatively related to one another (traditionally it is assumed that more risk should carry more reward for taking it on and vice-versa). He notes how this may have to do with the way in which institutional investors such as pension funds are structured organisationally, and how portfolio managers are compensated. This is one example of some interesting parallels in the behavioural finance field that could be drawn on.

A macroeconomic–microeconomic synthesis

Psychological factors have played a role in macroeconomic theory for decades now both at a general level and within the financial system especially. Concepts such as 'contagion' in banking and the 'propagation' of bank failures, which are primarily psychological and social in nature, are accepted in that domain as existing and having major impacts at the level of firm and system. This often justifies the use of large-scale fiscal and monetary policy responses.

And yet the acceptance of psychological dynamics in purely microeconomic settings is still piecemeal and sometimes only grudgingly admitted by the mainstream profession. At most, gentle 'nudges' are suggested as fixes and even the nature and content of these can stir up resistance.

This divide has many historical and ideological roots that are not of concern here. It should nonetheless be bridged by economists to allow for a freer development and application of findings, insights and ideas from the macroeconomic sphere into the microeconomic one and vice-versa. There is already a recognition with a micro institution such as the firm that the behavioural whole is often different than the sum of the parts. This must be integrated into the larger system in which the whole of firms in an industry or an economy are often different from their component parts.

Dynamic capabilities and key actor psychologies

Strategy formulation and execution are core tasks for any firm. The traditional management model has emphasised mainly the cognitive fitness, logic and rationality of the key actors, especially top executives, who carry these things out. And much of conceptualising is based on a static conception, e.g. where a firm is at a particular point in time.

In actual fact these individuals have their own psychologies, both individually and collectively, that have inordinate influence on the firm and its actions. And firms are dynamic, and the firm's capabilities are dynamic as well. Since personnel are a key component of institutional capabilities and since the individuals making up that personnel are often changing as well, a greater focus on these parts and their interaction is needed. Management theorists have been recognising this and incorporating psychology into how key Agents actually behave and believe and then integrating those insights into models of how these add up to and affect firm capabilities over time (Hodgkinson and Healey 2011).

There are examples of this sort of thinking in the economics realm as well. For example, Rajan and Zingales (1998) incorporate power – a traditionally sociological precept – into the transactions that take place in the firm, in this case represented by the regulation of access to critical resources. They note that access can be better than ownership. Meanwhile Bénabou and Tirole 2003, 2006) have examined the conflict between extrinsic motivation, in the form of incentives, and intrinsic motivation, as well pro-social motivation, and have integrated these within the formal modelling of actor behaviour that is so widely used in economics

The development of a catalogue of psychological effects as found in behavioural economics is very good and useful. But it may not be possible or advisable to simply generalise from these findings to the actions and decisions of key Principals and Agents in specific settings. And from a business strategy point of view the way in which actor psychologies blend into organisational capabilities is of critical interest. More attention should be paid to the psychological facets of key firm actors and how these flow into more general characteristics of the firm, such as capabilities.

An alternative paradigm: where to from here?

This chapter started with a discussion about the methodology of economics which traditionally is summed up in several criteria about what makes for the 'superior' theory. This can be recapped to say that the best theory is one that has: (1) congruence with reality; (2) generality; and (3) tractability and parsimony (Camerer and Loewenstein 2004: 4). Etzioni (2010: 379) refers to this as the conventional paradigm and says that it has three responses to behavioural economics: (1) ignore the findings; (2) claim the findings apply to only a limited or trivial set of choices; and (3) redefine rationality to incorporate the anomalies to explain them as 'optimal' (e.g. search costs as a justification for 'satisficing').

This indeed does seem to be a correct characterisation of behavioural economics and its relationship to mainstream economics. There are advantages to adding increments to a well-structured model like the neoclassical core. But the argument here is that while this approach is not per se a bad one, it is far too constrained and also too hampered by its own unexamined premises. An analogy could be made with old Ptolemaic model of planetary movement in which empirical observations contradicting the model's predictions were met with the addition of 'epicycles' to square model and reality. Until, that is, the Galilean/Copernican model overthrew it entirely with a sun-centred rather than earth-centred cosmos.

If behavioural findings are going to be applied to Corporate Governance Theory and policy in a robust way, we have to go beyond merely using 'precise functions that add one or two free parameters to standard rational theories [and] ... applied to explain important anomalies and make fresh predictions' (Camerer et al. 2003: 1216).

More needs to be openly discovered about that common element in all of this, the human being that inhabits the corporation and the nexus into which it fits. This is the 'ghost in the machine.' This obvious point has not been overlooked by scholars and practitioners but the humanity of the corporate actor still needs to be examined and understood more fully and integrated more centrally into the governance research and policy paradigm. True cross-, trans- and inter-disciplinarity is called for because no one viewpoint is complete. Which means letting of some generally treasured assumptions, certainly by economists and probably by others as well. The payoff is greater truth, so that is worth it.

A paradigm for future research in the field is offered here: that of the ecosystem. Rather than battle each other or fit into a hierarchy, different disciplines need to work symbiotically in ways that improve both the overall research and policy environment but also strengthen their individual species. A sort of methodological biodiversity would be achieved, with greater useful, usable and true knowledge the end result.

Figure 6.1 lays out a conceptual framework of how this might look for corporate governance. The construct – there are others – puts the neoclassical paradigm as a limited core and expands out from there to the broader currents in economics an on to other disciplines. No discipline need be replaced or supplanted (unless, of course, it is empirically invalidated completely) but each could contribute, waxing and waning as required. The boundaries of the various sets are of course subject to dispute and adjustment. This is not meant to be definitive but suggestive.

A lot of good work has been done but there is much yet to be accomplished. Hopefully this can be done more cooperatively than it has thus far.

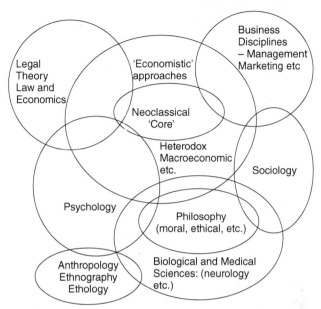

Figure 6.1 Conceptual framework of corporate governance

References

Agrawal, A. K., Catalini, C. and Goldfarb, A. (2013). *Some simple economics of crowdfunding* (working paper no. 19133). National Bureau of Economic Research (US).

Akerlof, G. and Shiller, R. (2009). *Animal Spirits: How Human Psychology Drives the Economy, and Why It Matters for Global Capitalism*. Woodstock and Princeton NJ: Princeton University Press (2009).

Alchian, A. A. and Demsetz, H. (1972). Production, information costs, and economic organization. *The American Economic Review*, 62 (December): 777–795.

Allen, F. and Gale, D. (2000). Financial contagion. *Journal of Political Economy*, 108(1): 1–33.

Anderson, K. (1978). Television fraud: The history and implications of the quiz show scandals. *Contributions in American Studies*, no. 39. Westport, CT: Greenwood Press.

Arcot, S., Bruno, V. and Faure-Grimaud, A. (2010). Corporate governance in the UK: Is the comply or explain approach working? *International Review of Law and Economics*, 30(2): 193–201.

Arrow, K. J. and Debreu, G. (1954). Existence of an equilibrium for a competitive economy. *Econometrica* (Journal of the Econometric Society), 22: 265–290.

Avgouleas, E. (2009). The global financial crisis, behavioural finance and financial regulation: In search of a new orthodoxy. *Journal of Corporate Law Studies*: 9(1), 23–59.

Avineri, E. (2012). On the use and potential of behavioural economics from the perspective of transport and climate change. *Journal of Transport Geography*, 24: 512–521.

Barber, W. J. (2010). *A History of Economic Thought*. Middleton, CT: Wesleyan University Press.

Barberis, N. and Thaler, R. (2003). A survey of behavioral finance. *Handbook of the Economics of Finance*, 1: 1053–1128.

Becht, M., Jenkinson, T. and Mayer, C. (2005). Corporate governance: An assessment. *Oxford Review of Economic Policy*, 21(2): 155–163.

Becker, G. (1976). *The Economic Approach to Human Behavior*. Chicago IL: University of Chicago Press.

Belleflamme, P., Lambert, T. and Schwienbacher, A. (2014). Crowdfunding: Tapping the right crowd. *Journal of Business Venturing*, 29(5): 585–609.

Bénabou, R. and Tirole, J. (2003). Intrinsic and extrinsic motivation. *The Review of Economic Studies*, 70(3): 489–520.

Bénabou, R. and Tirole, J. (2006). Incentives and prosocial behavior. *The American Economic Review*, 96(5): 1652–1678.

Besanko, D., Dranove, D., Shanley, M. and Schaefer, S. (2007). *Economics of Strategy*. Hoboken NJ: Wiley.

Binham, Caroline (2011). UK opens investigation into Olympus. *Financial Times*, 15 November. www.ft.com/cms/s/0/260aa57a-0fbd-11e1-a468-00144feabdc0.html#axzz 3dFLHCbAH [Accessed 16 June 2015]

Boulding, K. (1969). Economics as a moral science. *American Economic Review*, 59(1): 1–12.

Brabham, D. C. (2013). *Crowdsourcing*. Cambridge MA: MIT Press.

Boytsun, A., Deloof, M. and Matthyssens, P. (2011). Social norms, social cohesion, and corporate governance. *Corporate Governance: An International Review*, 19(1): 41–60.

Brickley, J., Smith, C., Zimmerman, J., Zhang, Z. and Wang, C. (2001). *Managerial Economics and Organizational Architecture* (Vol. 4). New York: McGraw-Hill/Irwin.

Brown, D. B., De Giorgi, E. G. and Sim, M. (2009). A satisficing alternative to prospect theory. Department of Economics, University of St. Gallen, Switzerland.

Burt, R. (1992). *Structural Holes: The Social Structure of Competition*. Cambridge MA: Harvard University Press.

Calavita, K., Pontell, H. N. and Tillman, R. (1997). *Big Money Crime: Fraud and Politics in the Savings and Loan Crisis*. Oakland CA: University of California Press.

Camerer, C. (1999). Behavioral economics: Reunifying psychology and economics, Proc Nat Acad Sci USA, 96 (September): 10575–10577.

Camerer, C. (2007). Neuroeconomics: Using neuroscience to make economic predictions. *The Economic Journal*, 117(519) Conference Papers. March: C26–C42.

Camerer, C., Issacharoff, S., Loewenstein, G., O'Donoghue, T. and Rabin, M. (2003). Regulation for conservatives: Behavioral economics and the case for 'Asymmetric Paternalism'. *University of Pennsylvania Law Review*, 1151(3): 1211–1254.

Camerer, C. and Loewenstein, G. (2004). Behavioral economics: Past, present, future. In C. Camerer, G. Loewenstein and M. Rabin (eds) *Advances in Behavorial Economics*. Princeton NJ: Princeton University Press, pp. 3–51.

Camerer, C., Loewenstein, G. and Weber, M. (1989). The curse of knowledge in economic settings: An experimental analysis. *The Journal of Political Economy*, 97: 1232–1254.

Cardenas, J. C. and Carpenter, J. (2008). Behavioural development economics: Lessons from field labs in the developing world. *The Journal of Development Studies*, 44(3): 311–338.

CBC News (2010). Timeline: Conrad Black through the years. www.cbc.ca/news/canada/ conrad-black-through-the-years-1.868133. [Accessed 22 May 2015]

Chandler, A. (1962). *Strategy and Structure: Chapters in the History of the American Industrial Enterprise*. Cambridge MA: MIT Press.

Cho, T. and Hambrick, D. (2006). Attention as the mediator between top management team characteristics and strategic change: The case of airline deregulation. *Organization Science*, 17: 453–469.

Choi, J. J., Laibson, D. and Madrian, B. C. (2004). Plan design and 401(k) savings outcomes (working paper no. 10486). National Bureau of Economic Research (US).

Clark, N. (2004). In the shadow of Vivendi scandal, ex-chief works to clear name. *New York Times*, 28 June 2004. www.nytimes.com/2004/06/28/business/media-in-shadow-of-vivendi-scandal-ex-chief-works-to-clear-name.html [Accessed 17 June 2015]

Coase, R. (1937). The nature of the firm. *Economica*, 4(16): 386–405.

Coffee Jr, J. C. (1998). Future as history: The prospects for global convergence in corporate governance and its implications. NW UL Rev., 93, 641.

Coffee Jr, J. C. (2001). Do norms matter? A cross-country evaluation. *University of Pennsylvania Law Review*, 149: 2151–2177.

Coffee Jr, J. (2006). *Gatekeepers: The Professions and Corporate Governance: The Professions and Corporate Governance*. Oxford: Oxford University Press.

Coffee Jr, J. (2011). Ratings reform: The good, the bad, and the ugly. *Harvard Business Law Review*, 1, 231. www.hblr.org/wp-content/uploads/2014/09/Ratings-Reform.pdf [Accessed 17 June 2015]

Conyon, M. J. (2014). Executive compensation and board governance in US Firms. *The Economic Journal*, 124(574): F60–F89.

Davern, M. T., Cummins, R. A. and Stokes, M. A. (2007). Subjective wellbeing as an affective-cognitive construct. *Journal of Happiness Studies*, 8(4): 429–449.

Davis, J., Schoorman, F. and Donaldson, L. (1997). Toward a stewardship theory of management. *Academy of Management Review*, 22(1): 20–47.

De Meza, D., Irlenbusch, B. and Reyniers, D. (2008). Financial capability: A behavioural economics perspective. London: Financial Services Authority. www.fca.org.uk/static/fca/documents/research/fsa-crpr69.pdf [Accessed 17 June 2015]

Denis, D. K. and McConnell, J. J. (2003). International corporate governance. *Journal of Financial and Quantitative Analysis*, 38(01): 1–36.

Docking, D. (2012). The 2008 financial crises and implications of the Dodd-Frank Act. *Journal Of Corporate Treasury Management*, 4(4): 353–363.

Dolan, P., Hallsworth, M., Halpern, D., King, D., Metcalfe, R. and Vlaev, I. (2012). Influencing behaviour: The mindspace way. *Journal of Economic Psychology*, 33(1): 264–277.

Dunning, J. H. (2013). *Multinationals, Technology and Competitiveness*. Abingdon: Routledge (RLE: International Business Vol. 13).

Edwards, F. (1999). Hedge funds and the collapse of long-term capital management. *Journal of Economic Perspectives*, 13(2): 189–210.

Epstein, R. (1983). Common law, labor law, and reality: A rejoinder to Professors Getman and Kohler. *Yale Law Journal*, 92(8): 1435–1441.

Ert, E. and Erev, I. (2013). On the descriptive value of loss aversion in decisions under risk: Six clarifications. *Judgment and Decision Making*, 8(3): 214.

Estellés-Arolas, E. and González-Ladrón-de-Guevara, F. (2012). Towards an integrated crowdsourcing definition. *Journal of Information Science*, 38(2): 189–200.

Etzioni, A. (2010). Bounded rationality. Discussion Forum II: Behavioural Economics, *Socio-Economic Review*, 8: 377–382.

Fama, E. (1980). Agency problems and the theory of the firm. *Journal of Political Economy*, 88(2): 288–307.

Fama, E. and Jensen, M. (1985). Organizational forms and investment decisions. *Journal of financial Economics*, 14(1): 101–119.

Financial Reporting Council (2012). Auditing Practices Board – Professional Scepticism: Establishing a common understanding and reaffirming its central role in delivering audit quality (March). www.frc.org.uk/Our-Work/Publications/APB/Briefing-Paper-Professional-Scepticism.aspx. [Accessed 22 May 2015]

Financial Reporting Council (2014). UK Corporate Governance Code. www.frc.org.uk/Our-Work/Publications/Corporate-Governance/UK-Corporate-Governance-Code-2014.pdf. [Accessed 22 May 2015]

Finkelstein, A. (2007). E-ZTax: Tax salience and tax rates, National Bureau of Economic Research. http://users.nber.org/~afinkels/papers/EZTax_Finkelstein_February_07.pdf [Accessed 24 June 2015]

Forbes, W. (2009). *Behavioural Finance*. Chichester: John Wiley & Sons.

Frankl, V. (2006). *Man's Search for Meaning*. Boston, MA: Beacon Press.

Frey, B. (1999). Morality and rationality in environmental policy. *Journal of Consumer Policy*, 22(4): 395–417.

Frey, B. (2001). Why economists disregard economic methodology. *Journal of Economic Methodology*, 8(1): 41–47.

Friedman, M. (1953). The methodology of positive economics. In *Essays in Positive Economics*, Chicago, IL: University of Chicago, pp. 3–43.

Frydman, C., Hilt, E. and Zhou, L. Y. (2012). Economic effects of runs on early 'Shadow Banks': Trust companies and the impact of the panic of 1907 (working paper no. 18264). National Bureau of Economic Research (US).

Galbraith, J. K. (2009). *The Great Crash 1929: The Classic Account of Financial Disaster*. Boston MA: Houghton Mifflin Harcourt.

Galbraith, J. R. and Kazanjian, R. K. (1986). *Strategy Implementation: The Role of Structure and Process* (2nd edn). St. Paul MN: West Publishing.

Gibbs, P. (Hiroshi, S.) (1996/1997): 'What is Occam's Razor?' www.math.ucr.edu/home/baez/physics/General/occam.html. [Accessed 22 May 2015]

Glimcher, P. W. and Fehr, E. (eds). (2013). *Neuroeconomics: Decision Making and the Brain*. Waltham, MA: Academic Press.

Gneezy, U., Meier, S. and Rey-Biel, P. (2011). When and why incentives (don't) work to modify behavior. *The Journal of Economic Perspectives*, 25(4): 191–209.

Grove, W. M., Zald, D. H., Lebow, B. S., Snitz, B. E. and Nelson, C. (2000). Clinical versus mechanical prediction: a meta-analysis. *Psychological Assessment*, 12(1): 19–30.

Hammond, T. H. (1996). Formal theory and the institutions of governance. *Governance*, 9(2): 107–185.

Haugen, R. A. (2003). The new finance: Overreaction, complexity, and uniqueness (3rd edn). London: Pearson College Division.

Hart, O. (2009). Hold-up, asset ownership, and reference points. *Quarterly Journal of Economics*, 124(1): 367–400.

Haugen, R. (1999) *The Inefficient Stock Market – What Pays Off and Why*. Upper Saddle River NJ: Prentice Hall

Hayek, F. (1945). The use of knowledge in society. *American Economic Review*, 35(4): 519–530.

Health Affairs Blog (2011). We're only human: Behavioral economics and British policy (Part 1), 11 July. http://healthaffairs.org/blog/2011/07/20/were-only-human-behavioral-economics-and-british-policy-part-1/. [Accessed 22 May 2015]

Heap, S. (2013). What is the meaning of behavioural economics? *Cambridge Journal of Economics*, 37(5): 985–1000.

Heimer, C. (2008). Thinking about how to avoid thought: Deep norms, shallow rules, and the structure of attention. *Regulation & Governance*, 2: 30–47.

Herring, R. J. (1993). BCCI: Lessons for international bank supervision. *Contemporary Economic Policy*, 11(2): 76–86.

Hertwig, R., Benz, B. and Krauss, S. (2008). The conjunction fallacy and the many meanings of *and*. *Cognition*, 108(3): 740–753.

Hodgkinson and Healey (2011). Psychological foundations of dynamic capabilities: Reflexion and reflection in strategic management. *Strategic Management Journal*, 32(13): 1500–1516.

Holmström, B. (1979). Moral hazard and observability. *The Bell Journal of Economics*, 10(1): 74–91.

Holmström, B. and Kaplan, S. N. (2001). Corporate governance and merger activity in the US: Making sense of the 1980s and 1990s (working paper no. 8220). National Bureau of Economic Research (US).

Holmström, B. and Kaplan, S. (2003). The state of US corporate governance: What's right and what's wrong? *Journal of Applied Corporate Finance* 15(3): 8–20.

Huse, M. (2005). Accountability and creating accountability: A framework for exploring behavioural perspectives on corporate governance. *British Journal of Management*, Vol 16 (supplement): S65–S79.

Jackson, G. (2010). Corporate Governance in the United States: An historical and theoretical reassessment. Hans-Böckler-Stiftung, Paper 223. www.boeckler.de/pdf/p_arbp_223.pdf. [Accessed 24 June 2015]

Jensen, M. and Meckling, W. (1979). *Theory of the Firm: Managerial Behavior, Agency Costs, and Ownership Structure*. Netherlands: Springer.

Jolls, C., Sunstein, C. and Thaler, R. (1998). A behavioral approach to law and economics. Standford Law Review, 50 (May): 1471–1550.

Kahneman, D. (2011). *Thinking, Fast and Slow*. New York: Macmillan.

Kahneman, D., Knetsch, J. L., & Thaler, R. H. (1986a). Fairness and the assumptions of economics. *Journal of Business*, 59, S285-S300.

Kahneman, D., Knetsch, J. L. and Thaler, R. (1986b). Fairness as a constraint on profit seeking: Entitlements in the market. *The American Economic Review*, 76(4): 728–741.

Kahneman, D. and Tversky, A. (1979). Prospect theory: An analysis of decision under risk. *Econometrica*, 47(2): 263–291.

Kaplan, S. N. (2012). Executive compensation and corporate governance in the US: perceptions, facts and challenges (working paper no. 18395). National Bureau of Economic Research (US).

Keen, S. (1995). Finance and economic breakdown: Modeling Minsky's 'financial instability hypothesis'. *Journal of Post-Keynesian Economics*, 17(4): 607–635.

Ketz, J. (2003). *Hidden Financial Risk: Understanding Off-Balance Sheet Accounting*. Hoboken NJ: John Wiley & Sons.

Kindleberger, C. and Aliber, R. (2011). *Manias, Panics and Crashes: A History of Financial Crises*. Basingstoke and New York: Palgrave Macmillan.

Kirkpatrick, G. (2009). The corporate governance lessons from the financial crisis. Financial Market Trends (OECD). www.oecd.org/finance/financial-markets/42229620.pdf [Accessed 16 June 2015]

Knight, F. H. (1921). *Risk, Uncertainty and Profit*. Boston, MA: Houghton Mifflin.

Knight, F. H. (1942). Profit and entrepreneurial functions. *The Journal of Economic History*, 2(S1): 126–132.

Kogut, B. and Zander, U. (1993). Knowledge of the firm and the evolutionary theory of the modern corporation. *Journal of International Business Studies*, 24(4): 625–645.

Korobkin, R. and Ulen, T. (2000). Law and behavioral science: Removing the rationality assumption from law and economics, *California Law Review*, 88(4): 1051–1143.

Labaton, S. (1986). Archives of business: A rogues gallery; Cortes Randell: student market hoax. *New York Times*, 7 December. www.nytimes.com/1986/12/07/business/archives-of-business-a-rogues-gallery-cortes-randell-student-market-hoax.html [Accessed 17 June 2015]

Lamoreaux, N. and Rosenthal, J. (2006). Corporate governance and the plight of minority shareholders in the United States before the Great Depression. In E. L. Glaeser and C. Goldin (eds) *Corruption and Reform: Lessons from America's Economic History*. Chicago, IL: University of Chicago Press, pp. 125–152.

Lazear, E. P. (2000). Economic imperialism. *Quarterly Journal of Economics*, 115(1): 99–146.

Lease, D. R. (2006). From great to ghastly: How toxic organizational cultures poison companies – the rise and fall of Enron, WorldCom, HealthSouth, and Tyco International. *Academy of Business Education*, April 6–7.

Lewin , S. B. (1996). Economics and psychology: Lessons for our own day from the early twentieth century. *Journal of Economic Literature*, 34(3): 1293–1323.

Lipman, F. (2012). From Enron to Lehman Brothers: Lessons for boards from recent corporate governance failures by Frederick D. Lipman, Director's Notes, The Conference Board (no. DN-V4N6) March.

List, J. A. (2006). Friend or foe? A natural experiment of the prisoner's dilemma. *The Review of Economics and Statistics*, 88(3): 463–471.

Loewenstein, G. (1999). Experimental economics from the vantage point of behavioural economics, *The Economic Journal* 109 (February): F25–F34.

Loewenstein, G., Asch, D. A., Friedman, J. Y., Melichar, L. A. and Volpp, K. G. (2012). Can behavioural economics make us healthier? *British Medical Journal*, 344(7863): 23–25.

Mackay, C. (1841/2002). *Extraordinary Popular Delusions and the Madness of Crowds*. New York: Barnes & Noble Publishing

MacKenzie, D. (2003). Long-term capital management and the sociology of arbitrage. *Economy and Society*, 32(3): 349–380.

MacNeal, K. (1939). *Truth in Accounting*. Philadelphia PA: University of Pennsylvania Press.

Maitlis, S. (2004). Taking it from the top: How CEOs influence (and fail to influence) their boards. *Organization Studies*, 25(8): 1275–1311.

Mallin, C., Mullineux, A. and Wihlborg, C. (2005). The financial sector and corporate governance: The UK case. *Corporate Governance: An International Review*, 13(4): 532–541.

Manne, H. (1965). Mergers and the market for corporate control. *The Journal of Political Economy*, 73(1): 110–120.

March, J. (1991). Exploration and exploitation in organizational learning. *Organization Science*, 2(1): 71–87.

Marnet, O. (2007). History repeats itself: The failure of rational choice models in corporate governance. *Critical Perspectives on Accounting* 18 (2007): 191–210.

Marshall, L. H. and Magoun, H. W. (2013). *Discoveries in the Human Brain: Neuroscience Prehistory, Brain Structure, and Function*. New York: Springer Science+Business Media.

McFadden, D. (2010). Sociality, rationality, and the ecology of choice. In S. Hess and A. Daly (eds) *Choice Modelling the State-of-the-Art and the State-of-Practice – Proceedings from the Inaugural International Choice Modelling Conference*. Bingley: Emerald Group Publishing, pp. 3–18.

McLean, B. and Nocera, J. (2010). *All The Devils Are Here: The Hidden History of the Financial Crisis*. New York: Portfolio/Penguin.

McQuillen, B. and Sugen, R. (2012). Reconciling normative and behavioural economics: The problems to be solved. *Social Choice and Welfare*, 38: 553–567.

Melis, A. (2005). Corporate governance failures: To what extent is Parmalat a particularly Italian Case? *Corporate Governance: An International Review*, 13(4): 78–88.

Mezulis, A. H., Abramson, L. Y., Hyde, J. S. abd Hankin, B. L. (2004). Is there a universal positivity bias in attributions? A meta-analytic review of individual, developmental, and cultural differences in the self-serving attributional bias. *Psychological Bulletin*, 130(5): 711.

Milgrom, P. and Roberts, J. (1992). *Economics, Organization and Management*, Englewood Cliffs NJ: Prentice-Hall.

Minsky, H. P. (1977). The financial instability hypothesis: An interpretation of Keynes and an alternative to 'standard' theory. Challenge, 20(1): 20–27.

Minsky, H. (1984). *Can 'It' Happen Again?: Essays on Instability and Finance*. Armonk, NY: ME Sharpe.

Minsky, H. (1995). Longer waves in financial relations: financial factors in the more severe depressions II, *Journal of Economic Issues*, 29(1): 83–96.

Minsky, H. (1996). Uncertainty and the institutional structure of capitalist economies. Working Paper no. 155, Jerome Levy Economics Institute of Bard College. www.levyinstitute.org/pubs/wp155.pdf [Accessed 17 June 2015]

Mitchell, A., Puxty, T., Sikka, P. and Willmott, H. (1994). Ethical statements as smokescreens for sectional interests: The case of the UK accountancy profession. *Journal of Business Ethics*, 13(1): 39–51.

Morck, R. (2008). Behavioral finance in corporate governance: Economics and ethics of the devil's advocate. *Journal of Managerial Governance*, 12(2): 179–200.

Morck, R. and Steier, L. (2005). The global history of corporate governance: An introduction. In R.K Morck (ed.) *A History of Corporate Governance Around the World: Family Business Groups to Professional Managers*. Chicago IL: University of Chicago Press, pp. 1–64.

Muldoon, M. F., Barger, S. D., Flory, J. D. and Manuck, S. B. (1998). What are quality of life measurements measuring? *British Medical Journal*, 316(7130): 542.

Mullaintathan, S. and Thaler, R. (2000). Behaviorial economics (working paper no. 7948). National Bureau of Economic Research (US).

National Archives (UK) (2014a). Explanatory notes to the Companies Act 2006. www.legislation.gov.uk/ukpga/2006/46/notes/contents. [Accessed 22 May 2015]

National Archives (UK) (2014b). Explanatory notes to the Enterprise and Regulatory Reform Act 2013. www.legislation.gov.uk/ukpga/2013/24/notes/contents. [Accessed 22 May 2015]

National Archives (UK) (2014c). The Large and Medium-sized Companies and Groups (Accounts and Reports) (Amendment) Regulations 2013. www.legislation.gov.uk/ukdsi/2013/9780111100318/schedule. [Accessed 22 May 2015]

Nelson, R. and Winter, S. (1982). *An Evolutionary Theory of Economic Change*. Cambridge MA: Belknap Press, pp. 72–136.

O'Brien, C. (2006). The downfall of Equitable Life in the United Kingdom: The mismatch of strategy and risk management. *Risk Management and Insurance Review*, 9(2): 189–204.

Ocasio, W. (1997). Towards an attention-based view of the firm. *Strategic Management Journal*, 18 (S1): 187–206.

OECD (2004). Principles of corporate governance 2004. www.oecd.org/daf/ca/corporategovernanceprinciples/31557724.pdf [Accessed 22 May 2015]

OECD (2005). OECD glossary of statistical terms. Entry on 'corporate governance', created 13 July 2005. www.oecd-ilibrary.org/docserver/download/3008121e.pdf?expires=1434549714&id=id&accname=guest&checksum=4EBBE23264C5CAE1380C48655103781D [Accessed 16 June 2015]

Ozkan, N. (2011). CEO compensation and firm performance: An empirical investigation of UK panel data. *European Financial Management*, 17(2): 260–285.

Paredes, T. (2004). Too much pay, too much deference: Behavioral corporate finance, CEOs, and corporate governance. Florida State University Law Review, (32) 673–762.

Piore, M. (2010). From bounded rationality to behavioural economics. Discussion Forum II: Behavioural Economics. *Socio-Economic Review*, (8): 383–387.

Pollitt, M. and Shaorshadze, I. (2011). The role of behavioural economics in energy and climate policy. University of Cambridge, Electricity Policy Research Group, EPRG working paper no. 1130, Cambridge Working Paper in Economics 1165.

Rajagopalan N. and Zhang Y. (2009). Recurring failures in corporate governance: A global disease? *Business Horizons*, 52(6): 545–552.

Rajan, R. G. and Zingales, L. (1998). Power in a theory of the firm. *The Quarterly Journal of Economics*, 113(2): 387–432.

Ramos, G. M., Daamen, W. and Hoogendoorn, S. (2014). A state-of-the-art review: Developments in Utility theory, Prospect theory and Regret theory to investigate travellers' behaviour in situations involving travel time uncertainty. *Transport Reviews*, 34(1): 46–67.

Reinhart, C. M. and Rogoff, K. (2009). *This Time Is Different: Eight Centuries of Financial Folly*. Princeton NJ: Princeton University Press.

Roach, L. (2011), The UK stewardship Code. *Journal of Corporate Law Studies*, 11(2): 463–484.

Roberts, J. (2004). *The Modern Firm: Organizational Design for Performance and Growth*. Oxford: Oxford University Press, pp. 32–67.

Roberts, R. (2008), Scandals and debacles, http://gale.cengage.co.uk/images/FT%20 Scandals%20and%20Debacles.pdf [Accessed 24 June 2015]

Roe, M. J. (ed.) (2005). *Corporate Governance: Political and Legal Perspectives* (Vol. 8). Cheltenham and Northampton MA: Edward Elgar Publishing.

Rubinstein, A. (1998). Similarity and decision-making under risk. Journal of Economic Theory, 46 (1988): 145–153.

Rubinstein, A. (2007). Instinctive and cognitive reasoning: A study of response times. *The Economic Journal*, 117(523): 1243–1259.

Salisbury, S. (1982), *No Way to Run a Railroad: The Untold Story of the Penn Central Crisis*. New York: McGraw-Hill Book Company.

Samuelson, P. A. (1937). A note on measurement of utility. *The Review of Economic Studies*, 4(2): 155–161.

Selten, R. (1998). Features of experimentally observed bounded rationality. *European Economic Review*, 42(3): 413–436.

Sen, A. (1970/1984). *Collective Choice and Social Welfare* (2nd edn). New York: Elsevier Science Publishing Co.

Sen, A. (1977). Rational fools: A critique of the behavioral foundations of economic theory. *Philosophy and Public Affairs*, 6(4): 317–344.

Shiller, R. J. (2015). *Irrational Exuberance*. Princeton NJ: Princeton University Press.

Shliefer, A. and Vishny, R. (1997). A survey of corporate governance. *Journal of Finance*, 52(2): 737–783.

Simon, H. (1955). A behavioral model of rational choice. *Quarterly Journal of Economics*, 69(1): 99–118.

Simon, H. (1957). *Models of Man*. New York: Wiley.

Simon, H. (1962). The architecture of complexity. *Proceedings of the American Philosophical Society*, 106(6): 467–482.

Simon, H. (1991). Organizations and markets. *Journal of Economic Perspectives*, 5(2): 25–44.

Smelser, N. J. and Swedberg, R. (eds) (2010). The sociological perspective on the economy. In *The Handbook of Economic Sociology*. Princeton NJ: Princeton University Press, pp. 3–26.

Smith, C. W. and Warner, J. B. (1979). On financial contracting: an analysis of bond covenants.

Journal of Financial Economics, 7(2): 117–161.

Smith, V. L. (2007). *Rationality in Economics: Constructivist and Ecological Forms*. New York: Cambridge University Press.

Spiller, P. (2008). An institutional theory of public contracts: Regulatory implications (working paper no. 14152). National Bureau of Economic Research (US).

Streeck, W. (2010). Does 'behavioural economics' offer an alternative to the neoclassical paradigm? Discussion Forum II: Behavioural Economics, *Socio-Economic Review*, 8(2): 387–397.

Stinchcombe, A. (1990). *Information and Organizations*, Berkeley CA: University of California Press.

Stiles, P. and Taylor, B. (1993). Maxwell – the failure of corporate governance. *Corporate Governance: An International Review*, 1(1): 34–45.

Subrahmanyam, A. (2008). Behavioural finance: A review and synthesis. *European Financial Management*, 14(1): 12–29.

Sundaramurthy, C. and Lewis, M. (2003). Control and collaboration: Paradoxes of governance. *Academy of Management Review*, 28(3), 397–415.

Tapia, W. and Yermo, J. (2007). Implications of behavioural economics for mandatory individual account pension systems, OECD Working Papers on Insurance and Private Pensions, no. 11, OECD Publishing.

Taylor, B. (2013). How the Salad Oil Swindle of 1963 nearly crippled the NYSE. Business Insider, 23 November 2013. www.businessinsider.com/the-great-salad-oil-scandal-of-1963-2013-11#ixzz3X7JtYoGe. [Accessed 22 May 2015]

Thaler, R. H. and Benartzi, S. (2004). Save more tomorrow™: Using behavioral economics to increase employee saving. *Journal of Political Economy*, 112(S1): S164–S187.

Thaler, R. and Sunstein, C. (2009). *Nudge: Improving Decisions About Health, Wealth and Happiness* (revised and expanded edition). New York: Penguin.

Tosi, H., Brownlee, A., Silva, P. and Katz, J. (2003). An empirical exploration of decision-making under agency controls and stewardship structure. *Journal of Management Studies*, 40(8): 2053–2071.

US Senate (2010). Brief Summary Of The Dodd-Frank Wall Street Reform And Consumer Protection Act. www.banking.senate.gov/public/_files/070110_Dodd_Frank_Wall_Street_Reform_comprehensive_summary_Final.pdf. [Accessed 22 May 2015]

Van Ees, H., Gabrielsson, J. and Huse, M. (2009). Toward a behavioral theory of boards and corporate governance. *Corporate Governance: An International Review*, 17(3): 307–319.

Vogel, T. J. (2001). Cendant Corp.: A case study examining the compensation and accounting issues involved in a Stock-Option Repricing Program. *Issues in Accounting Education*, 16(3): 409–441.

Watts, R. L. and Zimmerman, J. L. (1990). Positive Accounting theory: A ten year perspective. *The Accounting Review*, 65(1): 131–156.

Watts, T. (2002). A report on corporate governance at five companies that collapsed in 2001. August 2002, IA research. http://law.unimelb.edu.au/files/dmfile/Report_on_Governance_at_5_Failed_Companies_0310281.pdf [Accessed 16 June 2015]

Weisbach, M. S. (1988). Outside directors and CEO turnover. *Journal of Financial Economics*, 20(1–2): 431–460.

Wicker, E. (1980). A reconsideration of the causes of the banking panic of 1930. *The Journal of Economic History*, 40(03): 571–583.

Williamson, O. (1983). Organization form, residual claimants, and corporate control. *Journal of Law and Economics*, 26: 351–366.

Williamson, O. (1985). *The Economic Institutions of Capitalism*, New York: Free Press.

Williamson, O. (1988). Corporate finance and corporate governance. *Journal of Finance*, 43: 567–592.

Index

Entries in *italics* refer to titles of documents.